BASICALLY
MORELS

Mushroom Hunting,
Cooking, Lore & Advice

*For Lisa & Tom:
Happy hunting!
Larry McLoud*

What they're saying about **<u>BASICALLY MORELS</u>**...

BASICALLY
MORELS

Mushroom Hunting, Cooking, Lore & Advice

Larry Lonik

R K T PUBLISHING

Chelsea, Michigan 48118

BASICALLY MORELS:
Mushroom Hunting, Cooking, Lore & Advice

Second Edition, (2002)
First Printing
Copyright © 1999 by Larry Lonik
ISBN : 0931715-01-6

Portions of this book were previously published in The Curious Morel
© 1984, 1998 by Larry Lonik.

Visit our website **www.morelheaven.com** for more information about books and other products, photos & current information, Lonik's appearances, special events and more....

Every effort has been made to ensure that all information, including images and opinions, is accurate and current. However, the author and publisher cannot accept any responsibility for loss, injury, illness or inconvenience, however caused, related to the content of this book.

R K T PUBLISHING

CHELSEA, MICHIGAN 48118

For my father

"If you can't go first class...don't go."

Contents

Introduction

Every May the State of Michigan is invaded by an army of 600,000 fanatics who arrange their only vacation time from their regular employment so they can dress in old clothes, carry sticks and bags, wander deliberately but haphazardly away from cities and road, kick through brambles and swamps, brave cold and rain, battle mosquitoes and spider webs, keep to themselves, invariably prevaricate when confronted by other human beings and hold festivals to celebrate their bizarre rituals. These people are drawn, zombie-like, into orchards, fields and forests, over rivers and hills in search of tiny sponge-like growths that are as unpredictable in habit as they are difficult to spot. License plates from as many as a dozen other states and Canadian provinces can be found on cars parked along two-rutted paths that are little more than bear trails in the middle of virtual nowhere.

The reason? The air is cool and clean. The woods and meadows are alive with the sights and smells of beautiful wildflowers. The soil is fresh and rich.

All of nature is shaking off the cobwebs of another long, continuing winter. Newborn animals and birds frolic innocently. The activity is healthy and invigorating. The search itself... the guessing... the perseverance...the luck...is thrilling. These things all add to the pleasure of this special, limited season, but the overriding draw is the delicious meaty flavor of the object of all this attention: the morel mushroom.

Michigan has long been a target of morel fanciers but, in fact, morels can be found in most areas of the United States and Canada. <u>Basically Morels</u> will detail how to find morels wherever you live: where to look, when to look, festivals, clubs and organizations that offer additional assistance and enjoyment. It explains what morels really are and how to differentiate them from other kinds of mushrooms. The state of Michigan is

often used throughout the book as an example area. Most areas have organized hunting activities, literature and, at least, morels themselves. With a little investigation and application all the information herein is accurate and practical.

<u>Basically Morels</u> is also legends, lore, opinions, suggestions, advice and pictures (including exclusive photos of cultivated morels). However, the most enjoyable section of the book, as the most enjoyable part of morel hunting, has to do with eating. Enjoyment of a hard-earned find is a pleasure to the palate. Dozens of recipes, many from fine reataurants and festi-

This amazing photograph shows some of the first morels ever grown indoors – obviously outside of their natural habitat - under controlled, laboratory-like conditions. Wild morels grow rapidly in the wild, but much slower in controlled environments. Many attempts to grow morels (indoors and outdoors, in various places around the globe) have been documented over the last 50 years. There has been progress and breakthroughs, but not to the point that they are available, fresh, every day in large quantities.

val contests, are included to ensure ultimate exultation in your culinary endeavors, be they simple or sophisticated.

You might wonder what stimulated me to invest nearly twenty years in research in order to present the proverbial "everything you ever wanted to know" about morel mushrooms. Well...not so very long ago I found myself talking to a fellow, a stranger, who seemed quite rational and mature until we got on the subject of morels. His eyes seemed to light up, his speech energetically intensified and his mannerisms became excitedly exaggerated. I found it quite fascinating. He had not missed a season since his father introduced him to morel hunting when he was only six years old. For richer and for poorer, in sickness and in health, for 30 consecutive years he was drawn, at times almost in a trance, to the fields and forests of Michigan. He lived and worked in the Florida Keys for two years but found excuses (admitting the real reason to no one but himself) to make the 30-hour drive to the Great Lakes State at the end of April. Even at the southern-most part of the U.S., 1,500 miles from melting snows and the end of winter hibernation, his "inner calendar" told him of the excitement that nature would soon present in his native state.

He talked tirelessly of "The Hunt", with such enthusiasm that I was ready to slip into my hiking boots and ask a grocery store clerk for a dozen large bags. He showed me the long-strided low walk he claimed was the most efficient way to productively cruise a woods. It reminded me of Groucho Marx. He told me how the morels "hid" and sometimes even ran away, so when you found one you should keep perfectly still and quiet as you crouched next to it, carefully pinching it off just above the ground as you scanned the area. They almost always traveled in groups, he said, and one of the biggest thrills was trying to find where the captured morel's buddies were. If you made noises, he warned me, they would

scurry away in the camouflage. With systematic stealth you had to comb the area, knowing they were nearby but not gonna go easily. Sometimes, he said, if you were really, really, really lucky you could come upon what must have been an entire morel convention - a sight...an emotion...unparalleled in all of life as we know it. He told me that he found such a "convention" about five years back. He and a friend picked, on their knees, continuously for nearly three hours, acknowledging and appreciating each and every trophy. They took off their shirts and filled them, made three trips, of over two miles each way, to the car. Later, after they ate all they could and spread the rest on screens to dry, he figured the spot had been good for about 90 pounds! He never found another spot like it and, when he returned the following year, not only did he not find even one, he also got arrested for trespassing—even though it was State land.

The "mushroom walk" is a long, low stride morel hunters use to move quickly, yet alertly, through fields and woods. If you're not finding mushrooms in an area, no matter how well it fits the ideal hunting ground "mold", keep moving.. The low profile or "the walk" is maintained to more advantageously outline morel caps against the background.. Eyes should be focusing ten to fifteen feet ahead while walking.

He closed his eyes at one point, squeezing them tight. He said that after you find a few morels in the woods, you can close your eyes and they'll appear, as clear as a photograph, in your head - not the memory of one you've already picked, but a new one, one you've never seen before. Sometimes, he said, it made sleeping a bit difficult, especially if the day's huntin' was good.

And he told me about the side of morel hunting that wasn't all fun. He'd been lost (usually every year, he said sheepishly), caught in snowstorms, hypothermia - threatening cold rain, his vehicle stuck miles from civilization (another annual occurrence), walking 20 miles a day and finding nothing for weeks, mosquitoes, flies, swamps, thistle, thorns, spider webs, running out of gas and tearing off exhaust systems. He went north to a secret remote spot once, had a tooth abscess the first day, and stayed five

sleepless, painful days and nights, sleeping (not sleeping, actually) in the back of a small car (the guy was six-foot-seven!) Fortunately, it was a mushroom - productive five days and he managed to preserve 70 pounds for the up-coming off-season. Unfortunately, though, the dried morels were destroyed - about $1,200 worth - when his parents' house (where they were stored) burned down. He explained that it wasn't all fun, but it was enjoyable.

This fellow, who seemed quite usual until morels were mentioned, seemed to detect I was beginning to get some reservations about his overall mental state. He did seem a bit fanatical about this one particular subject. Then he told me why. He, above all, loved to eat morels. The smell. The taste. The texture. Again he closed his eyes. They tasted like the finest steak imaginable, he said. But delicate. A little chewy. A little wild. A little nut-like. A dreamy, lost look came over him and I knew why he, ultimately, had never missed a season since his father had first informed him and his brother that the last one to find a morel each year was a "monkey's uncle". The great healthy exercise, the beautiful sights and rich smells of Nature awak-ening and stirring, the thrill of the always new and unpredictable treasure hunt, and one of the most exquisite tastes on Earth. And all for free! I was hooked. I was excited. I was ready.

Then I opened MY eyes. The guy who was telling me about the won-ders, mysteries and mania of morel mushroom hunting was not a stranger. I was talking to myself, reminding myself of my own morel experiences over 40 seasons. And I never will miss a season. My passion for this particu-lar experience transcends the obvious joys and rewards. I'm very grateful I was introduced to this fascinating activity and have been given the oppor-tunity to encourage and assist others in the delightful and delectable ways of The Curious Morel.

Enjoy.

A very special tip of the mushroom cap to:

Cathy, Vonnie and Virginia Howard, Brian Broker, Dr. Everett "Tex" Beneke, Fred Trost, the "Practical Sportsman" cast and crew, Herb Harper, Mike Trout, State of Minnesota, Sen. Gary Laidig, Rep. Phyllis Kahn, Colleen Wahl, Joan Huyser, NAMA, Ken Cochran, Joe Miller, the immaculately obscure Joy, Harry Knighton, Timothy Hickey, "Scout" Fred Urbshott, Tony Fleischmann,, the Hope Bay Gang, Lenny Zulewski (G-Man), State of Michigan, Department of Natural Resources, Larry Meyer, Michigan Retailers' Association, Michigan State University, Boyne City, Bookcrafters, Anne and Roseanne, Rachel, Chuck Russell, Dave and Kay Richey, Gina and Norman Anselment, Lesley Pritchard, MUSHROOM the Journal, Don Coombs, Tom and Vicky Nauman, Gwen Simmons, Robin McGraw, Bunker Hill, Neogen, Dr. Miller, Dr.Willis Wood, Dr. Gary Mills, Jim Malachowski, John Hull, Lynn Morgan, Brian Bishop, Jane Starley, Anthony and JoAnn Lonik, Gary and Debbie, Barry and Lara (Treemores XIV), Great Grandmother Lawrence, the entire Lawrence family, my boys Jason, Hans, James Michael, Stevie, Crimson and King, my girl Stephanie Reed, Linda and Charlie Irons, Lex and Sherry Maples, Ron, Karla, Susan, Susan, Chris Carl, Lina & Rich Blaut, Melissa and Pat at the Graphics Factory, Detroit Entreprenurial Institute, Jim Utley, The Mr. Mushroom family, Gary Mack, George and Carolyn Parent, Bartolo, George Cunningham and the Fillin' Station Gang, Dr. Ray Davis, Gino and Cathy Sabolcik, Terese Treemore, and Squonks everywhere. Stay curious.

PART ONE

The Morel:

Fungus Amungus

I. WHY

Motives,

Festivals & Organizations

Fifty million people on the planet Earth actively seek the elusive wild mushroom known as the morel. The explanation is really quite simple. The morel is the most easily recognized and most desirable in flavor and texture of all mushrooms. It is thought of with the highest regard in the very best cookery. In Europe especially, but also in Asia, the traditions of the annual morel hunt span generations. Favorite hunting spots are kept secret, guarded like family heirlooms through the ages. The inhabitants of North America have more recently, but with great avidity, been swelling the ranks of one of the world's great outdoor activities. And no wonder. Morel hunting is a wonderful family activity. And it's easy!

Trillium

There's no special equipment involved. People of all ages, sizes and shapes can enjoy searching for, picking and eating morels. There's no license needed (at least not yet). Location is no particular barrier. Local parks, public land, forests, woodlots, fields and yards often are conducive to morel production. There is no special training other than a few basic hints and precautions. As easily as one recognizes basic flowers and trees, and as readily as one deduces which wild berries are edible, morels can be distinguished. There is no risk eating wild mushrooms of proven quality - kinds

that have been consumed safely and pleasurably in many lands for thousands of years. There is danger in eating wild mushrooms indiscriminately. Morels, in particular, can be recognized with ease and certainty and are positively known to be good, edible and choice.

Following basic rules and common sense they are delicious, wholesome and as safe as any wild vegetable, though less nourishing than most. To those that know and like them, their flavor more than makes up for their lack of nourishment. Indeed, their low caloric content is a positive attraction to many. That precise fact is one of the main reasons there is great interest in developing a method of growing morels commercially. Imagine – a rich, meaty flavor and texture with practically no calories!

ALWAYS use a mesh bag when collecting mushrooms.
It allows the mushrooms to breathe, but most importantly,
allows spore (the reproductive structure of mushrooms)
to return to the woods and fields. Similar to the tale of
Johnny Appleseed, one can actually "seed" areas for more
mushrooms in the future.

WWW.MORELHEAVEN.COM

*The bag I like best is a soft mesh bag that doesn't abrade
the mushroom, allows good air circulation and drops
spores while you're walking. An excellent example is the
"Spore Boy" bag, available from the website*
www.morelheaven.com
*This bag was developed specifically for mushroom col-
lecting: soft yet sturdy, with handles, beltloops and a self-
storage pouch—convenient and effective.*

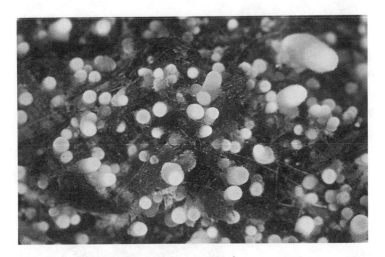

*Morel mushrooms have recently been grown in a labo-
ratory and, on a limited basis, commercially. This
exclusive photo, showing an early stage of the morel
growth cycle reveals what are known as fundaments,
the very beginnings of the "fruit bodies". The laboratory morels grow much more gradually, about one cen-
timeter per day, than wild morels, which seem to
instantly "pop" to their ultimate dimensions. True commercial development and availability to the general
public are still a few years away, but the feat thought
impossible for centuries and attempted so many times,
has indeed become a reality.*

Extended commercial production could replace, or at least challenge,
the substance we generally classify as "meat". Laboratory tests with animals have already borne out the fact that the protein content of morels is
sufficient to sustain life.

Mushrooms, primarily the common button type (Agaricus bisporus),
are already big business. In 1995 North American commercial production
topped the <u>one billion pound</u> mark for the first time. The Kennett Square

area of eastern Pennsylvania contributes about 40% of that total. And compared to morels they're pretty tasteless....

The list of organized activities devoted to or concerned with morel (and other mushroom) hunting in North America is rapidly lengthening since the Boston Mycological Club first met on Saturday, August 24, 1895. 100 years later, today, more than 25,000 mushroomers are actual members of amateur clubs and societies that publish newsletters and sponsor weekend hunts. The following list reveals a geographic diversity strung loosely together by a common thread: the interest in, and study of, fleshy fungi....

ALASKA-Southeast Alaska Mycol. Assn. (Sitka)
ARKANSAS~Arkansas Mycol. Soc. (Pine Bluff)
ARIZONA-Arizona Mushroom club (Mesa)
CALIFORNIA-Fungus Federation of (Santa Cruz); Humboldt Bay Mycol. Soc. (Arcata); (Los Angeles) Mycol. Soc.; Mycol. Soc. of (San Francisco)
COLORADO-Colorado Mycol. Soc. (LaFayette); Pike's Peak Mycol. Soc. (Colorado Springs)
CONNECTICUT- Conn. Valley Mycol. Soc. (Trumbull)
FLORIDA-Gulf States Mycol. Soc. (Port Walton Beach)
IOWA-Prairie States Mushroom club (Pella)
IDAHO-North Idaho Mycol. Assn. (Hayden); Palouse Mycol. Assn. (Moscow); Southern Idaho Mycol. Assn. (Boise)
ILLINOIS-lllinois Mycol. Assn. (Franklin Park)
KANSAS-Kaw Valley Mycol. Soc. (Lawrence)
MASSACHUSETTES-Boston Mycol. Club (Maynard)
MARYLAND-Lower Bast Shore Mushroom club (Princess Anne)
MAINE-Maine Mycol. Soc. (Bowdoinham)
MICHIGAN-Michigan Mushroom Hunter's Club (Redford); West Michigan Mycol. Soc. (Ludington)
MINNESOTA-Minnesota Mycol. Soc. (Edina)
MISSOURI-Missouri Mycol. Soc. (Ballwin)
MONTANA-Southwest Montana Mycol. Assn. (Bozeman); Western Montana Mycol. Assn. (Missoula)
NORTH CAROLINA-(Asheville) Mushroom Club; Blue Ridge Mushroom Club (North Wilkesboro); Cape Pear Mycol. Soc. (Leland)

Triangle Area Mushroom Club (Durham)
NORTH DAKOTA-Fun Gis Mycol. Assn. (Mandan)
NEW HAMPSHIRE-Monadnock Mushroomers Unlimited (Keene); New
Hampshire Mycol. Soc. (Nashua)
NEW JERSEY-New Jersey Mycol. Assn. (Denville)
NEW MEXICO-New Mexico Mycol. Soc. (Albuquerque)
NEW YORK- O.M.A. (Pound Ridge); Long Island Mycol. Club
(Northport); Mid Hudson Mycol. Assn. (Modena); Mid York Mycol.
Soc. (Clinton); New York Mycol. Soc. (NYC); (Rochester) Area
Mycol. Assn.; Susquehanna Valley Mycol. Soc. (Endicott)
OHIO-Ohio Mushroom Society (Concord)
OREGON-Lincoln County Mycol. Soc. (Lincoln City); North American
Truffling Society (Corvallis); Oregon Mycol. Soc. (Milwaukie)
PENNSYLVANIA-Eastern Pennsylvania Mushroomers (Lancaster)
SOUTH CAROLINA-South Carolina Chapter of NAMA (Cleveland)
TEXAS-Texas Mycol. Soc. (Houston)
UTAH-Mushroom Soc. of Utah (Salt Lake City)
VIRGINIA-Mycol. Assn. of Washington (Syria)
VERMONT-Vermont Mycol. Club (Burlington)
WASHINGTON-Kitsap Peninsula Mycol. Soc. (Brenerton); Northwest
Mushroomers Assn. (Bellingham); Puget Sound Mycol. Soc. (Seattle);
Snohomish County Mycol. Soc. (Everett); South Sound Mushroom
Club (Olympia); (Spokane) Mushroom Club; (Tacoma) Mushroom
Society; Wenatchee Valley Mushroom Soc. (Monitor)
WISCONSIN-Wisconsin Mycol. Soc. (Mukwonago)
WEST VIRGINIA-West Virginia Mycol. Assn. (Elkins)
ALBERTA-Romonton Mycol. Soc. (Edmonton)
BRITISH COLUMBIA-South Vancouver Island Mycol. Soc. (Brentwood
Bay); (Vancouver) Mycol. Soc.
ONTARIO-Mycol. Soc. of Toronto (Uxbridge)
QUEBEC-Cercle des Mycologues de (Montreal); Cercle des Mycologues
du Saguenay (Chicoutmi); Cercle Mycologues de (Quebec)

I highly recommend these organizations for their expertise and cama-
raderie. In my dozens of experiences at club outings and meetings I've
found the people genuinely welcoming and willing to share their knowl-

edge. I suggest contacting NAMA (North American Mycological Association) for the current contact information of a club near you.

Website: www.namyco.org
North American Mycological Association
10 Lynn Brooke Place
Charleston, WV 25312-9521

Mushroom festivals are another source of information and fun. Many areas hold these celebrations annually, claiming themselves as National, International or World Capitals. These fests usually offer parades, guided tours, taste samples, seminars, arts and crafts, recipe contests, games, rides, mushroom maps and morel picking contests. The mushroom picking championships have contestants pay a small entry fee to be bused or led caravan-style to a secluded, protected, proven-productive forest. For 90 minutes they race around, trying to find the most, largest or smallest morels. There are usually divisions for resident and non-residents, men and women. Sometimes there are "runoffs" and winners get cash or prizes. Over the years Boyne City, Michigan winners recorded anywhere from 15 to 945 morels. (The contestants DO get to keep their mushrooms). Some examples of U.S. morel festivals....

Illinois—Magnolia (1st Sat./May), Jonesboro (3rd weekend/April),
     Farmington (2nd Sat./May)
Indiana—Mansfield (last weekend/April)
Michigan—Mesick (40 +years, week ending with Mother's Day), Boyne
     City (39 yrs, weekend after Mother's Day), Cadillac, Lewiston
Wisconsin—Muscoda (third weekend of May)
Pennsylvania- -Redding

Minnesota—Elba (Mother's Day weekend)
Missouri—Richmond
British Columbia/Canada—Salmon Arm Morel Festival (first week/
    June)
Also: Washington, Oregon, Alaska, New York, Utah, Minnesota and
    more, with an annual growing list....

Check with State Tourist Bureaus, NAMA or the clubs for more information.

I've surveyed people at morel festivals, asking the obviously avid mushroomers what morels tasted like. A few of the answers might give

novice hunters a hint of what to expect if they are successful....

"The finest, thinly-sliced sirloin steak."
"Delicate."
"Chewy."
"Steamed, fresh clams."
"Tender."
"The King of Mushrooms."
"All other mushrooms are bland in comparison."
"After a day in the woods, like gold."
"Delicious."

The last statement is not far from the truth. Morels, in season, can be purchased, if they can be found, for $10-$30 per pound. Out of season, they can only be acquired from specialty stores. In their dehydrated state <u>one ounce</u> (which will become 1/2 pound after soaking in water) sells for $10-$20, or $160-$320 per pound of dried morels.

The combination of the truly enjoyable healthy activity, the fabulous flavor and the exorbitant monetary value of morels lead to one more unique truth about this sport. If you ask questions of anyone during morel season (How's the hunting? Where are you finding them?), remember: all mushroom hunters lie.

Dogwood

II. WHAT

Fungi,

Mushrooms & Morels

The highly-prized, fervently-sought morel mushroom is not a mushroom. In a vast, complicated world of varied organisms all mushrooms are fungi. Morels also, are fungi but do not technically fit the scientific definition of "mushroom". That fact, however accurate, is insignificant to the millions of people who annually scour the countryside for one of the tastiest treats of the natural seasons. They're going to hunt, pick and eat morels no matter what they're called. The distinctions really aren't important, but an essential understanding of the forms of life that morels are does shed some light on where and when to find them.

The entire fungus world is strange and unnatural to most people. The sound of the word "fungus" and its connotations are repulsive to many. The mere existence of fungi seems an odd phenomenon— many types appear rapidly (overnight) and are gone soon after. Rain often seems to trigger their growth, growth that is astonishingly fast and mysterious. They seem to be at the mercy of their environment. In reality, however, the world would be one gigantic garbage dump if it were not for fungi. Fungi decompose decaying matter. The forest floor would be covered with fallen trees and leaves if fungi did not aid in breaking them down into re-usable substances. They are vital in reforestation, especially of blighted areas, and in management of ecosystems. Contrary to the popular belief that fungi are a lower form of life and have a relatively simple existence, most are exquisitely constructed and their life cycles are among the most complex found anywhere in nature. In their evolution from single-celled organisms they have lost (or perhaps never had) the ability to photosynthesize that most plants have. A great diversity in the fungi kingdom make categorization difficult. The higher forms of fungi follow similar patterns of growth. Ascomycetes and basidiomycetes, which include morels and mushrooms, are among these higher forms.

The growing, or vegetative, part of a mushroom is hidden in the ground. The mushroom, as seen from above ground, is the fruit body of the plant. Its function is to produce the greatest number of spores in the shortest possible time and release them into the atmosphere. When the released spore lands on the ground, it seeks moisture and food. A protuberance elongates into a filament called a "hypha". The hyphae continue to grow and when filaments of two compatible strains come together, they connect and divide, eventually forming a dense network of underground fibers called a "mycelium" (plural, mycelia). The span of life of these mycelia is measured in years, decades and even centuries. Year after year the mycelia lie dormant in winter and dry periods, but quickly become active when conditions are again favorable. The elaborate fruiting structures, what we see, pick and eat as mushrooms are the fruit of the entire fungal system of an area.

Bolete or Cep

Because fungi have no chlorophyll they cannot make their own food. Nutrients must come from the Soil, dead leaves, trees and other types of organic material. Decaying vegetable matter encourages fungal growth. Grassy places and forests are favorable environments, mushrooms, generally seem to grow best in older, wooded areas.

Chanterelle

Mycelia can also cause decay, and decay in standing or falling trees is evidence of existing mycelia. Because of soil conditions, these networks often extend in "veins", thus explaining patterns of growth often evident when picking morels. A usually reliable rule states, "When you find one, look around. There's probably more nearby."

Though there is no typical life cycle of a fungus, they are grouped by the way they generate spores for reproduction. Basidiomycetes produce spores on a club-like structure. The fruiting structures of this group are greatly varied in size and shape. Mushrooms are basidiomycetes.

Another large group of higher fungi are the ascomycetes. They are distinguished by a unique sac-life reproductive structure call an "ascus". The asci (plural) stand on end, packed tightly together like a dense carpet, and cover the surface of the fruiting cap. Morels, which reproduce by means of asci are ascomycetes and, therefore are technically not mushrooms.

There are over 200,000 known species of mushrooms or fungi in the world, ranging from one-celled organisms that grow in ponds to giant puffballs big enough to sit on. They come in all forms, looking like heads of cauliflower, coral, slabs of beefsteak, sponges, umbrellas and icicles. Some even glow in the dark. Many are a treat for the tastebuds. About 30 are picked for use in cooking. Others can cause discomfort and a few (about 40) are known to be deadly. In the United States only half a dozen species of 10,000 are deadly, with about five related fatalities reported each year. Toxins in some mushrooms may affect the central nervous system, about 6-10 hours after eating. Others cause gastrointestinal irritation, within one-half to three hours after consumption. You should avoid eating mushrooms that have a cup around their base and are all white, including the gills. The

"Destroying Angel" follows that description, but there is no simple or fool-proof way to distinguish harmful from harmless mushrooms. There seems to be an inconsistency in books and great confusion in identification. Yet, around the world, mushroom consumption and interest has dramatically increased.

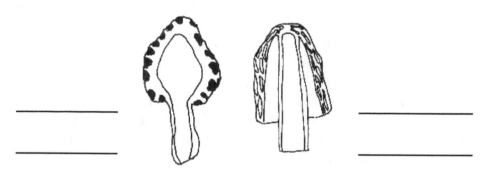

Cross-sections of a true morel (Morchella) and a false morel (Verpa). The stalk of the true morel is hollow and joined to the bottom end of the cap. The stalk of the false morel may be hollow or pithy and is attached only at the top of the cap.

Shoppers in France can routinely choose from among 20 species of mushrooms in their marketplace. 30 varieties are available in Finland. Heavy sales are being reported in all of Europe, India and China. In North America, methods of gathering and marketing fresh wild mushrooms have advanced. Armies of food gatherers scout woods in places such as Washington, Oregon, California, British Columbia, Alaska and Michigan, harvesting edible fungi. They are carefully placed in cartons and flown around the world. Names such as morel, bolete, shiitake and chanterelle are becoming more well-known are accepted in restaurants, markets and homes.

Many local supermarkets in America offer European dried mushrooms, usually chanterelles or boletes, which go by the names of "Polish" or "imported" mushrooms.

The cultivated mushroom sold in groceries is the <u>Agaricus bisporus</u>. It is offered in three grades: small (immature specimens called "buttons"), medium ("cups") and large ("open" or "flat"). The demand for more varied and exotic mushrooms has spurred the consumer to look beyond the <u>Agari-</u><u>cus</u>. Several varieties of wild mushrooms grow in most parts of the United States and Canada. Morels are the most popular, followed by puffballs, chanterelles, shaggymanes, boletes, shelf and stump mushrooms.

Puffballs (<u>Calvatia</u>) appear predominantly in September and October during periods of high humidity. They are usually found in open areas-lawns, pastures, golf courses. They taste like eggplant and are usually eaten sliced and fried. The giant puffball (<u>Calvatia maxima</u>) can get as large as three feet in diameter. Several varieties of puffballs can be found, all are edible unless their skin is tough.

(Chanterelle, © Larry Lonik)

Chanterelles are yolk-colored and trumpet bell-shaped, usually ready for harvesting from August to October. They are delicate and supposedly appear after a temperature dip following the high point of summer heat. Their flavor is thick and meaty, with a faint apricot taste.

Shaggymanes are considered the best of the inky-cap group. They have egg-shaped, shiny, smooth caps. They have gills and the young specimens have a narrow, loose ring around the stem at the edge of the cap. The ring later withers and disappears. They grow to heights of up to 20 inches, in groups on lawns, in parks and in fields. You should avoid alcohol consumption with shaggymanes as they have been known to magnify the effects of the alcohol.

Oyster mushrooms are shell-shaped white fans that grow on one side of tree trunks or logs. Meadow mushrooms are closely related to the common (<u>Agaricus</u>) button and can be found in horse pastures. Boletes (or ceps) are considered the Number One wild mushroom in Central Europe. The flavor is sweet and nutty. They are available in dried form at many markets. Other mushrooms "out there" include stump ("honey") mushrooms, sulfur shelf fungus and fairy ring mushrooms. The safest way to enjoy all wild mushrooms is to study, use a field guide, and initially hunt with an experienced guide (such as a mushroom club). Mushrooming is safe for the sensible, dangerous for the careless or ignorant.

The most popular target of the world's wild mushroomers is the morel. The stem and the cap are the fruit of the plant that lies underground, enmeshed in the soil. What lies below the surface is the "apple tree". The morels are the apples. They contain no chlorophyll as do ordinary green plants, so they are dependent on existing supplies of food. If temperature and moisture are adequate, they will flourish as long as their nutritional needs are met. And morels are picky about their food. To understand what their food sources are, and where these sources can be found, is a great advantage in locating morels.

Morels are known by a variety of names in addition to their botanical classifications. Among the non-scientific terms are: "blacks", "whites", "blondes", "grays", "pit-heads", "skirts", "coneheads", "Spring mushrooms", "brains", "sponge mushrooms", "Johnny Jump-ups", "beefsteaks", "big foot", and "club foot". Indeed, there are many types of morels, both "true" and "false". Some mycologists claim to have identified more than 60 species. Usually they are simplified into three or four. The common names can become quite confusing so a description of the different types, by scientific (Latin) designations is the most accurate breakdown of the variety of morels. Collectors are advised to learn these basic classifications for general identification as well as any problems that might arise. The Latin descriptions consist of two words, the group (genus) followed by the particular type (species). The genus is capitalized. The book MORELS: TRUE OR FALSE is a practical field guide for morels. It contains color photos of the true and false morels in their natural habitat and cross-sections for positive identification.

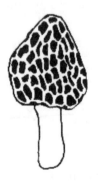

The exteriors of a true morel (<u>Morchella</u>) and a false morel (<u>Verpa</u>). The true morel has deep, dark irregular pits. The stalk is light- colored and is joined to the bottom of the cap. The false morel has longer, vertical ridges. The stalk is also light-colored, but disappears into the cap and is attached, skirt-like, at the top of the cap.

Morchella is the group name of "true" morels. False morels are commonly known as "lorchels". The Verpa genus, Gyromitra and Helvella genus are regarded as lorchels. All of the morels, both true and false, fruit most heavily in the Spring. In Michigan, the season may start as early as the latter part of April and continue to as late as early June. In areas of the Pacific Northwest the season may start in April and continue through July, with higher elevations producing staggered harvests.

True morels (Morchella genus) vary considerably in size and color, but they do have common characteristics that make them distinguishable from all other fungi. They have a more-or-less cone-shaped head, connected at the base of the head to a white or cream-colored stem. Both stem and cap are hollow. The second main distinction of all true morels is the pitted surface of the head. The pits may vary in shape and shade, but they always look like gouges were taken out of the cap. Morels can be found in a variety of environments but, very generally, they look like miniature Christmas trees poking out of the leafy forest mat.

False morels (lorchels) have stalks, that are attached directly to the top of their caps. The caps may flare out like a bell or A-line skirt or be puffy with the connection hidden inside the rolls of the cap. The caps, which hang free, may be fairly smooth, wrinkled, puffed or folded. The stalks themselves may be hollow or filled with a cottony substance Verpa and Gyromitra look like brains, saddles or skirts atop stalks that are long or hardly visible. They are sometimes called "elephant ears", "bull nose", "brains", "saddle mushrooms", "liver mushrooms", "skirts", "bells", "umbrellas" and "beefsteaks". No false morels, however, have caps which are "pitted", as do the members of the Morchella genus.

TRUE MORELS.

The first morel to "pop" out is <u>Morchella angusticeps</u>. They are a slender species, two to five inches in height, often with a pointed cap. The pits in the cap are longer than wide, forming vertical ridges. The colors range from pale tan to black, darkening as the mushroom ages. They are generally known as "black morels", are a hardy species and are considered excellent and choice for eating.

Black morels. Notice the variance in size and shape as well as how the caps are attached to the stems.

The "white morel", <u>Morchella esculenta</u>, appears after the first blacks but often their presences overlap. They vary in color from pale tan to yel-low to light orange to gray, and in shape from cone-like to chubby or roundish. The pits on the head are deep and irregularly spaced. They often resemble, in hue and pattern, a sponge. They are three to five inches high, solid to the touch, excellent and choice for eating

The giant morel, usually six to eight inches in height but recorded as tall as eighteen inches, is the last of the three basic true morels to appear. <u>Morchella crassipes</u>, often called "big foot", has a large, cone-shaped head and a thick stalk, sometimes wider at the base. The pits are irregular but rounder than the black morel's longitudinal hollows. Quite similar to <u>Morchella esculenta</u> (except for size), they are not as common as <u>esculenta</u> but are excellent and choice for eating.

Some people recognize other species of morels (including <u>Morchella deliciosa</u>, <u>Morchella hybrida</u>, <u>Morchella semilibera</u>, <u>Morchella elata</u>, <u>Morchella bispora</u> and <u>Morchella conica</u>). I concede the existence of a greater variety than blacks, whites, and giants, but for practical purposes I believe such a simplification is more than adequate. The differences include morels that are albino-like white, dark with white ridges, black throughout its lifetime and stems that are attached just above the bottom of the cap. All have pits. All are hollow. All caps are attached basically in the same manner to their stalks. All are true morels. All are exquisite to eat.

FALSE MORELS

One of the most prevalent of the lorchels, during morel season, is the
Verpa bohemica. Often called the "skirted morel" or "bell mushroom" it is
a prime example of the difference between true and false morels. It has an
overhanging cap with long vertical ridges, attached at its top to the stalk.
The stalks may be hollow or "pithy" (containing a cotton-like substance).
The caps are tan to yellowish brown, the stalks cream-colored. It is one of
the most visible species in the forest, standing erect, four to eight inches
tall. Though this is not a true morel, it is considered a "morel" by most. It is
counted as a "good" mushroom at many festival picking contests and sold
at roadside stands during plentiful seasons. Officially, though, it is considered "questionable" for eating. It does smell like a morel when fresh, and
tastes like a morel when cooked. Most people pick and eat them with no ill
effects.

During the 1977 morel season, most of the morels I found were of the
Verpa bohemica variety. Upon returning home, I cooked about 40,
primarily bohemicas, for dinner, using my favorite basic recipe (see BASIC
BACON AND MORELS). About an hour after thoroughly enjoying my
meal, I noticed a slight lack of muscular coordination. When walking through
a doorway, my arm seemed to brush the frame I thought I was easily clear
of. Several doorways, and bumps, later, I began to notice that everything I
looked at seemed to have a "glow" to it. The overall feeling was pleasant
enough, a little similar to being cheerfully tipsy from "one drink too many".
I only became a bit concerned when I realized that I didn't know what the
cause was. Perhaps it was the onset of a more serious disorder... I tele-
phoned the Biology Department at Michigan State University and described the situation to Dr. Everett Beneke, a plant pathologist. Dr. Beneke
explained that the Verpa bohemica can have a slight muscle-relaxing property that may manifest itself if eaten in a considerable quantity. The "glow"

I visually experienced was due to relaxed eye muscles that allowed more light into my dilated pupils. An hour later I was back to normal, though a little wiser. I have never found the skirted morels in that quantity since.

<u>Verpa bohemica</u>, the skirted morel. This is not a true morel. The cap hangs free. It is still considered a morel by most people, counted as a morel in festival picking contests, sold with other morels (in good years) at roadside stands. It smells and tastes like other morels, but one shoutd be cautious with this type. It does have a slight muscle-relaxant property that, when eaten in large amounts, can result in a state similar to drunkenness.

The <u>Gyromitra esculenta</u> is another lorchel that is commonly eaten though current classifications regard it as unsafe. Called the "beefsteak morel", it appears early in the season, is two to eight inches high, tan to "liver" in color and has a great variation in size and surface texture. The cap may be smooth, wrinkled or billowy, but never pitted. The stalk is usually hollow. It smells like a fresh morel and tastes like a morel. It does, however, contain the poison monomethylhydrazine. Though often eaten with no adverse reaction, the toxin may be cumulative, even over a considerable period of time (years). Deaths directly and definitely attributed to <u>Gyromitra esculenta</u> have been recorded. Prolonged cooking in an uncovered pan is strongly recommended if one chooses to disregard warnings and eat the beefsteaks. The fumes, while cooking, should not be inhaled.

<u>Gyromitra gigas</u> is a heavy, solid mushroom similar in appearance to <u>Gyromitra esculenta</u>. The edibility designations of this mushroom are typically inconsistent. One publication lists it as "good for eating". Another says it is not recommended. One real advantage of looking for true morels is that, once you know what you're looking for, there's nothing that resembles them. Two other species of <u>Gyromitra, infula</u> and <u>underwoodii</u>, are definitely poisonous. I recommend not eating any of the Gyromitras or Helvella

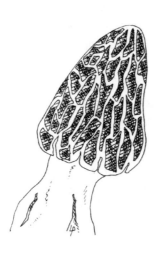

The biggest problem you will encounter when collecting morels will be not finding them. Most morel hunters, unfortunately, will come home empty handed. The experience, still, is tremendously enjoyable. Be careful about what you pick and when you pick. If you have any questions or doubts about your find, there are usually authorities not too far away to aid in identification. In Michigan, for example, the Cranbrook Academy of Science in Detroit and the University of Michigan Herbarium offer such services.

III. WHERE

Topography

The most frequently asked question by uninitiated, novice and seasoned morel enthusiasts alike is "Where do you find them?" Probably the most accurate answer is "Almost anywhere". Morels are very unpredictable. They may be abundant in a particular location one year and yield none the following season. I have personally experienced a three-year drought followed by the best crop I've ever seen, looking in exactly the same places! Guesswork, perseverance and luck do have a lot to do with successful mushroom hunting.

As part of the survey I made at several mushroom festivals in Michigan in 1983, I asked "Where have you found morels?" The answers, in no particular order:

"Aspen stands."
"Swampy areas."
"Hardwoods."
"Birch trees."
"Pine trees."
"Cedar trees."
"Along river beds."
"Open fields."
"Dense, older forests."
"Golf courses."

"Cemetaries."
"Along fencerows."
"Along roads."
"Stumps."
"Elm trees."
"Near fresh water."
"In light snow with sunshine."
"As far away from civilization as possible."
"In the backyard."
"Hillsides."
"In the sunshine."
"In the shade."
"Near wild raspberry bushes."
"Mostly in the Upper Peninsula of Michigan."
"Never in the Upper Peninsula of Michigan."
"Very tops of steep hills."
"The most inaccessible places."
"Young, second-growth hardwood."
"Orchards."
"Spruce stumps."
"Ash trees."
"Following ravines."
"Along power lines."
"Light, rolling hills."
"Recently burned-over areas."
"Deep grasses."
"Around trilliums."
"Where dogwood blooms."
"Near fiddlehead ferns."
"Near leeks."
"In the rocks along the shores of Lake Michigan."
"In moist, rich, dark soil."
"In dry leaves."

"Around forest decay."
"Along railroad tracks."
"South-facing slopes."
"At the base of slopes."
"Maple trees."
"Mixed hardwood stands."
"Edge of puddles."
"Conifer stands."
"Melting snowbanks."
"Balsam trees."
"Oak trees."
"Around cement steps."
"Elms dead ten years or more."
"Elms dead four years or less."
"Moist valleys."
"Paths."
"By old garages."
"Near old sumps."
"Deep in prickly ash."

Morels can be found in every state of the United States and every province of Canada, as well as around the world. Timing is critical, though, as the morel season is relatively short. When to look for morels will be discussed in detail in the next chapter. There do seem to be some prevailing physical conditions that should be kept in mind when choosing a potential morel hunting ground. The morel plant, in mycelial form, requires years, even decades, to develop. Once it is developed, however, it takes years (or decades) to dissipate, so one key to locating morels is to find an area that is "older" - one that show signs of past and continuing life cycles. Older trees, stumps, leaves and decay are evidence of a long and healthy existence. Elm trees are a recurring clue given by successful mushroomers.

Sometimes morels can be found in the most unlikely places.

The 45th parallel is definitely in THE MOREL ZONE..

All of the responses to my question (Where have you found morels?) I believe were true statements. The answers were all categorical, not very specific. I would never believe specific-location advice given by a mushroomer. From my own experience and research I know that morels can pop up just about anywhere. As the progression of morel species runs its cycle, however, different environments seem more conducive to their development.

Morchella angusticeps, the black morel, appears first in the season. Good places to look would include hardwood forests, aspen stands, mixed stands, apple orchards and along roadsides.

The white morels, Morchella esculenta, follow the blacks by about a week. They are usually in moister, richer earth, near streams and lakes. Stands of ash trees, dead or dying elm trees and apple orchards are other likely areas to find these lighter colored, often easier-to-spot morsels.

The giant morels, Morchella crassipes, are the third and last of the edible and choice morel species, appearing about a week after the whites. These "big foots" are associated with richer soil and warmer climate. Rich, moist valley streams, rich garden soil, under ash and elm, in orchards and in heavy grasses are all potential picking places.

The fever strikes all people and establishments in THE MOREL ZONE.

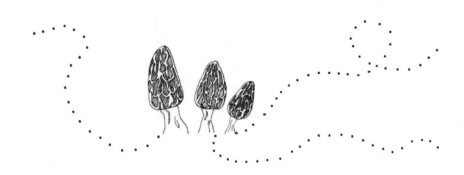

IV. WHEN

Time & Weather

Morels fruit in the Spring when the first wildflowers bloom. They appear first in the southern climates of the United States and make their elusive way north at the rate of about 100 miles per week. The season in any particular area lasts approximately 3 weeks, with a slightly more extended span northward. Altitudes, temperatures and the Jet Stream all play important roles in determining the specific "whens" of morel appearances across North America. Many of the warmer U.S. states begin their seasons as early as February. One could conceivably follow the morel migration northward for six months or more, ending up in the Yukon (Canada). A sampling of areas and their respective picking seasons...

Southern California	-	February
Louisiana	-	March
Northern California	-	March-May
Carolinas	-	March 15-April 15
Washington, DC	-	April 20-May 10
Northeast U.S.	-	May
Midwest U.S.	-	April 10-May 30
Pacific Northwest	-	April 20-August 30
Northern U.S.	-	May 20-June 30
Canada	-	May 15-August 30

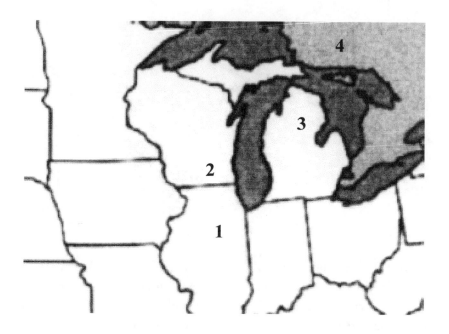

Morel mushroom picking times. The season lasts approximately three weeks (in any one spot), with the blacks, whites, then giants appearing in succession. Morels "travel" about 100 miles, northward, per week. They can be found from Georgia to the north of Canada, from California to Maine. On this map, morels may first appear in Section 1 around the middle of April and can be found through the first week of May. Section 2 would have a season of late April to middle May. Section 3, the month of May. Section 4, middle May to middle June. The seasons will vary with the weather (temperature and moisture), but generally the 100 miles per week applies. I've tested this theory many times, over small and great distances, with success.

Using Michigan as an example, the black morels appear in early May and they can be found during the following ten to fourteen days. White morels come "out of hiding" about a week after the first blacks. Their existence continues about ten days. The giant morels force themselves away from the underground morel plant and into the atmosphere about a week after the first whites have appeared. Their stay is a little shorter, a week at the most. The blacks are probably the hardiest of the Big Three. They start the earliest, sometimes even in snow. Their life span is the longest. The warming trend of Spring seems to be the trigger. Warmth, humidity (moisture) in the proper nutritional setting will (should) result in the fruit of the morel plant (what we pick) maturing. It is this very same combination of warmth and humidity that leads to the morels' demise. A warm Spring rain will push morels through the forest floor, but a continuation of those conditions will lead to their deterioration. Ideally, a (1) hot humid day, followed by (2) cool, dry days and nights would (1) start the morels growing and (2) freshly preserve them. They do not last long though. Even in the ideal situation they will last only three to five days. Moisture is the culprit - a second warm Spring rain will wipe out an existing crop. A cold, dry Spring can mean almost total failure for the entire year.

The white morels (<u>M. esculenta</u>), appearing a bit after the blacks, are therefore exposed to slightly milder weather, quite possibly explaining their shorter range of existence. The giants (<u>M. crassipes</u>) have the shortest lives and appear the latest. They also are the biggest. But, for all morels, just as quickly and mysteriously as they appear, they're gone.

Morchella crassipes, *just before picking. Note the mushroom is beginning to dry. Higher temperatures outside (maybe 75 degrees F.) and a higher moisture content of the mushroom itself contribute. Soaking in cool water for an hour before cooking will help return the proper moisture and make the mushroom less "tough".*

Survey Question Number Three read, "When have you found morels?" These responses (in Michigan, remember) included:

"In April."
"In May."
"In June."
"After warm Spring rains."
"When the earth first smells rich, moist and clean."
"Two weeks either side of Mother's Day."
"Around the time of the mushroom festivals."
"Two weeks after the mushroom festivals."
"The first time the thermometer hits 65."
"When the wildflowers bloom."

"When apple trees blossom."
"When oak leaves are as big as squirrels' ears."
"When the first asparagus spears are up."
"When hepatica, arbutus and white violets are blooming."
"Opening day of trout season."

Morel season is a great time to view and photograph the many wild-flowers that grace field and forest. Not only are they delicate and beautiful but they also can be morel indicators. The trillium, as seen on the book cover and in artwork throughout, is a perfect example. Many wildflowers are not to be picked, though they may be abundant. They are "protected" and should not be disturbed that others may long appreciate their beauty. Some of these Spring flowers include: Flowering Dogwood, American Lotus, White Trillium, Purple Trillium, Variegated Trillium, Climbing Bittersweet, Spring Beauty (Arbutus), Holly, Purple Fringed Orchid, Lady's Slippers, Trailing Arbutus, Trout Lily (Adder's Tongue), "May Apple", wild straw-berry, Jack-in-the-Pulpit, Birdfoot Violet, Prince's Pine, Club Mosses, Gen-tians. These can be found in the state of Michigan but many are evident across the country, along with a multitude of others not found in Michigan.

You can expect to see more than fabulous flora marking the end of winter. Birds are nesting. Newly born squirrels, chipmunks, owls, deer and other animals are quite often nearby. Man is the intruder in nature's won-derland and he should move with due respect for the privacy of animals and plants that abound.

The perpetual abundance of beauty and vitality always make an outing in morel season an exciting and worthwhile adventure. Morels, some-times, seem to be an excuse (although a very good excuse) to get out and enjoy Nature's wonders. It is very important, also, to respect the rights of property owners. Never trespass on private land without previous permis-sion. Instances of vandalism and violence have, unfortunately, been in-creasing along with the numbers of mushroom hunters. There is a great amount of public land (forests, preserves, recreation areas, state and national properties) to legally and safely explore. Public land, of course, also deserves your respect. Maps from states, counties, Chambers of Commerce, Natural Resources departments, etc., are available to aid prospective foragers in selecting safe sites. Most often these protected areas offer vast acres of prime potential picking.

On May 1, 1984, 1, the "Practical Sportsman" (Midwest television show) camera crew and host Fred Trost tramped through the woods in order to film an actual morel hunt. In addition to the unpredictability and elusiveness of morels, we faced the odds of it being extremely early in the picking season, having to search for morels in an area that was absolutely unknown to all of us, with little notice, to be completed in just a few hours, for a broadcast two days later. My only hunting experiences around the Lansing, Michigan area were generally unsuccessful — to the point that I never searched Lansing for my serious wild mushroom needs.

For one full hour we found nothing but a variety of beautiful wildflowers and a playful baby horned owl while we hauled and dragged cameras and equipment through brambles, thistles, grabby pinchy raspberry bushes, over fallen trees and through swamps. Finally, in a low flat area a crew member looked down and spotted a little dark cap pushing through the dry leaves by his foot. The first morel of the season! 15 feet away- another. Three. Four. Ten. Then a lull. We all stooped low (even the cameraman), looking for the little gems they had never seen until the last five minutes and I hadn't seen for eleven months. The excitement bubbled as we scoured the area, not saying a word, hardly moving. "There's one!" We scrambled, though very cautiously, to the vicinity, constantly and diligently searching the forest floor. It reminded me of children in an Easter egg hunt... and the first time I found morels.

Later, on a separate segment for the "Practical Sportsman" program, we cooked and ate the 40 or so morels we found on May 1. In a taste test we sautéed half in butter and half with bacon. Upon sampling, the four judges immediately and emphatically voted: two for butter, two for bacon.

I did have other opportunities to hunt the Lansing area and my opinion changed by finding ample amounts in several locations for personal consumption and small gifts.

V. HOW

Hunting,

Hints & Precautions,

Publications

Collecting morels can be a most gratifying and productive outdoor hobby when pursued in a safe manner according to the rules of the game. A genuine respect for plants and animals and an honest regard for property, both public and private, are especially important in any outdoor activity - and mushroom hunting is no exception.

Don't expect to find morels easily, especially at first. They blend into the grass and leaves and often look exactly like stumps, twigs and shadows. Though you may not succeed initially, be assured that your "eye" will improve with practice. Getting closer to the ground sometimes helps. Bending over, kneeling or doing the "mushroom squat" may aid your perspective by providing a background more conducive to outlining the distinctive morel shapes. A particular low stride, often known as "the mushroom walk", is sometimes recommended. It combines the lower eye level, focusing ten to fifteen feet ahead, with a variable pace, usually faster than walking. It's a good idea NOT to stay in an area too long, even though the conditions look perfect, if you're not finding morels. The mushroom walk enables the hunter to cover more territory while maintaining a closer-to-the-ground perspective. The walk appears to be an unnatural movement and, in fact, is strenuous exercise that should be avoided by those with physical restrictions. Mushrooming does entail considerable bodily exertion. The terrain is uneven and varied, often difficult. You will encounter pesky plants and pesty insects. Be forewarned and prepared.

The "mushroom squat". When you find a morel, there most likely are others nearby. Sit still and look around. Be careful not to step on any. The lower perspective is recommended. Children, because of their shorter stature, often make great mushroom hunters.

Mushroom hunting is one of the least expensive of all outdoor sports. No special equipment is needed. There is no license to procure. Comfortable clothes and a receptacle in which to place your find are the basic requirements, although certain preparations will make your outing safer and more enjoyable.

Wear comfortable, preferably old, clothes. Long pants and long sleeves are highly recommended to prevent direct exposure of your skin to threatening plants (brambles, poison ivy, etc.) and insects. Be aware of the irregular weather that has tremendous variance at this time of year. In Michigan, it can be 70 degrees or snow. Shoes should be waterproof and comfortable. If you wear glasses or contact lenses, wear your glasses. Protective eyewear (plastic safety shield) can be worn to keep errant branches and spider webs out of the eyes. Wearing hand protection (garden gloves) and a hat can be advantageous.

Carry an onion sack or some type of mesh bag. There are now mesh bags specifically designed to help protect your harvest and allow spore to be released back into the forest. This is particularly important when you're hunting areas you want to go back to year after year as predictable, favorite spots. The "Spore Boy" bag is an excellent example of a bag designed with all these considerations. Air circulation and avoidance of moisture are essential in keeping your morel catch fresh. Never use a plastic bag. Never put your find in a warm or humid place (car trunk, for example). Morels will deteriorate rapidly if not kept cool and dry after they are picked.

A walking stick (brought or easily found at most foraging sites) can be of assistance in clearing paths, as a walking aid, as a wet-area probe and for moving grasses and leaves in your pursuit. I also, always bring a camera.

Use other rules of common sense dictated by the activity you are undertaking. Since you will be in unfamiliar territory, it is wise to bring maps and a compass, and a whistle. For the same reason it is a good idea to never go mushrooming alone. A small pack with food and water can be very helpful. Bring a watch and keep track of time, allowing ample return time. Be sure to have plenty of gasoline in your vehicle. A chain or a winch and tools offer additional insurance, as some of the "less-than" roads in the Spring can be treacherous.

Now that you know precisely and positively what you're after and have properly prepared for a safe and successful excursion, a few more hints and precautions will enable you to best pick, prepare and preserve any and all morels you are fortunate enough to come across.

Some suggest having scissors or a sharp knife to snip morels off just above the ground. It is important to not disturb the mycelium by pulling the mushroom entirely from the ground, but pinching the very base of the stem, carefully and cleanly, is probably sufficient. Keep your collection as free from dirt as possible. Morels, amazingly, push through the forest floor with no loose soil or grit on them. Try to keep them that way.

Collect only one species at a time. If you do find more than one type, keep them separate. Keep only fresh, young specimens. Morels are best at the peak of their maturity (when they first appear). Clean, prepare and process mushrooms as soon as possible. They will deteriorate rapidly after they are picked. They can be kept for a few days by refrigerating in a sealed container.

Eat only a small amount of any one variety that is new or questionable. Some edible mushrooms can cause allergic reactions. In my research I have come across a number of statements and opinions, many contradictory. One, in particular, professed that all mushrooms contain some kind of toxin by nature and should be cooked. Another said that one out of one hundred people can be expected to have an allergic reaction (nausea, vomiting, cramps) to morels. I agree that all wild mushrooms should be cooked. Many are indigestible when raw. Morels are rarely eaten by rabbits or deer in the forest. Occasionally little nibbles are taken out of a morel by a young rabbit or squirrel, but not totally devoured. This to me at least, is a good indication that morels should not be eaten in their natural state. If animals DID eat morels regularly, we'd have an even tougher time getting any.

I do, unfortunately, have personal proof that some people should not eat morels. My younger brother became ill with severe cramps that last time he ate them. He had eaten them safely for years and we shared the same morels-in-spaghetti-sauce meal the night he became (very) ill. He had reached his "tolerance" level somehow. He still loves to venture into the woods and pick morels, but won't try them again, no matter how they're prepared.

The first time you eat a wild mushroom, eat sparingly. Observe any reaction you might have. Always save a few fresh specimens for identification just in case you become sick. Tolerances are individual and varied. Each person should record their own reactions. Avoid overeating. Toxins may be cumulative and reach a "saturation point" before manifesting themselves. Cooked mushrooms should not be re-heated or eaten at a later time. Do not drink alcohol while, or after, eating certain kinds of mushrooms. Alcohol extracts a toxin from shaggymanes and other inky-cap mushrooms that can cause symptoms similar to drunkenness and/or drowsiness. Don't eat mushrooms picked next to busy highways. They may contain herbicides or metals from vehicle exhaust.

One on-going source of information about morels and other wild edibles is <u>Mushroom, The Journal of Wild Mushrooming</u>. It is published four times a year. For subscription and/or advertising information write: Mushroom, Box 3156 L, University Station, Moscow, Idaho 83843.

Another good way to prepare for an initial morel hunt is to take a mushroom identification course at a high school, college or university. Go with an experienced mushroom hunter if at all possible and take a reference guide. Several publications are available from libraries, book stores, extension services of universities, local and state governments. Orson Miller's <u>Mushrooms of North America</u> and Dr. Alexander Smith's <u>Mushroom Hunters' Field Guide</u> are good field references. In the state of Michigan, several pamphlets are available through the Extension Bulletin Office (P.O. Box 231, East Lansing, Michigan 48824) of the Michigan State University Extension Service. They include:

"May is Morel Month in Michigan."

"Mushrooms Grow on Stumps."

"Wood Waste Makes Wonderful Mushrooms."

"Best of the Boletes."

"Don't Pick Poison When Gathering Mushrooms for Food in Michigan."

The Department of Natural Resources of the State of Michigan also has an interesting and informative pamphlet on "Spring Wildflowers and Mushrooms." Most states and provinces offer some sort of publication to assist their constituents in finding and identifying wild mushrooms. Check your area.

With respect for the rules of safety and propriety, morel hunting is in the same class as boating, fishing, game hunting, camping and other outdoor activities. You, too, can be one of those bent-over figures, looking as if you've lost your grandmother's diamond, calling out in triumph as you spot your treasure. The elation will come naturally.

This is the largest morel I ever saw, picked and ate.
It was growing near railroad tracks in a Detroit suburb.
It measured 14 inches tall and was delicious.

PART TWO

So You Found
Some Morels . . .

I.

Drying,

Freezing & Canning

After a successful mushroom outing, you'll want to know just what to do with your precious discovery. There are two choices: eating them and saving them.

If you have been fortunate enough to have a surplus, there are several methods of preserving them to enjoy throughout the year. I like drying them, though others claim success and preference in freezing and canning. In any case, the notion of relishing these rare and tasty morsels throughout the year is mouthwatering.

There are four ways to dry morels, depending on location and available equipment. All achieve the desired result. Always keep morels as clean as possible. Remove any dirt from the stems. Do not wash.

One convenient and simple method of drying morels is sewing them together with needle and thread or fishing filament. String them up in the sunshine with good air circulation. Four to eight hours later, they will be considerably shriveled and brittle. Remove the strings and place the mushrooms in bags or jars to store. Keep them in a cool, dry place. They will last years. This is a great way to preserve your morels, especially while camping. Be careful not to allow drying or dried mushrooms to get wet, either from rain or early morning dew. They will discolor and disintegrate quicklly after they've dried.

Dried morels on a 9-inch paper plate.

A second method of drying morels, that also can be used outdoors, is using a nylon screen. Raise the mesh on blocks of wood or logs to allow air to circulate around the mushrooms. Place the screen in direct sunlight for best results. Drying time and storage directions are the same as stringing them. Do not use a metal screen as it can cause oxidation and discoloration.

If you bring your mushrooms home soon after picking them, they can be dehydrated in an oven. Place the clean morels, not overlapping, in shallow pans. Place in oven at a low temperature, with the door ajar. Drying should be completed in about 45 minutes. Watch closely and remove to cool when brittle and wrinkled.

The relatively new fruit and vegetable dehydrators can be used to dry morels. Follow unit's directions. Experiment. I've had excellent results with some machines, particularly if I cut the morels in half.

Drying a large morel find on a nylon screen. Put in direct sunlight and raise to allow for air circulation. 12 pounds of freshly picked morels were on the screen. They dried to 1 1/2 pounds in about 8 hours. Do not leave out overnight as increased humidity or dew will spoil the mushrooms.

MOREL QUIZ

Answer "T" if true of all "true" morels:

T	F	1.	Cap pitted and Sponge-like
T	F	2.	Cap wavy with brain-like wrinkles
T	F	3.	Cap partially wrinkled and smooth
T	F	4.	Cap saddle-shaped
T	F	5.	Cap skirt-like
T	F	6.	Cap white, yellow, gray
T	F	7.	Stem attached to top of cap
T	F	8.	Stem attached at bottom
T	F	9.	Stem hollow
T	F	10.	Stem brownish
T	F	11.	Stem pithy or cottony
T	F	12.	Found throughout Summer
T	F	13.	Found during a few weeks around Spring
T	F	14.	Tastes meaty
T	F	15.	Tastes like a good grade of cardboard.
T	F	16.	Can cause an allergic reaction

List scientific names:

_____   17.   *White morel*

_____   18.   *Skirted morel*

_____   19.   *"Big Foot" morel*

_____   20.   *Black, early morel*

Answers on next page.

The ratio of fresh morels to dried morels is 8:1. I store my dehydrated mushrooms in two ounce packages. They will hydrate back to one pound. To restore dried morels, place them in cool water for at least one-half hour (some people use warm water or milk), or until fully soaked. They will return to their original shape, size and weight (minus a degree of initial rigidity). Gently squeeze out the excess water by hand. They are ready to use. I think they taste just as good as fresh morels. Some people feel drying actually improves the flavor and dissipates toxicity. In any case, enjoying morels in the middle of a cold winter stirs both the taste buds and memories of enjoyable Spring days.

Morels can be frozen for future use. One method is to cut the morels in half (lengthwise), wash, then cook until covered with their own juices. Air cool or set pan in cold water. Pack mushrooms, with juice, into containers, leaving about one-half inch of space at the top. Seal and freeze at zero degrees Fahrenheit or below. The most popular method used by restaurants is to half-sauté them in butter and a little onion (do the onion first, fried until "clear", then add the mushrooms). Cool slightly, then put into heavy plastic bags or containers. Into the freezer they go. When you go to use the frozen morels, heat a frying pan to medium-high heat. Put frozen product directly into the pan. <u>Do not thaw first!</u> This will minimize the possibilityof the morels being "tough" when prepared.

Morel Quiz Answers

1.T   2. F   3. F   4. F   5. F   6. T   7. F.   8.T 9.T
    10. F   11. F   12. F   13.T   14. T   15. F   16. T

17.   *Morchella esculenta*
18.   *Verpa bohemica*
19.   *Morchella crassipes*
20.   *Morchella angusticeps*

A second method involves steam blanching. Cut the morels into small chunks. Immerse in a solution of one teaspoon lemon juice (or 1-1/2 teaspoons citric acid) per pint of water. Soak for five minutes. Remove mushrooms and steam three to five minutes. Cool in cold water. Drain. Pack in containers.

Freeze.

A third way to preserve morels by freezing involves no heat. Soak whole morels in cool water for one-half hour with six teaspoons of salt. Remove. Pat dry with paper towels. Pack and freeze. Hint: when using frozen morels in cooking, directly add them to your recipe. Do not thaw frozen morels as they will become "rubbery" (but still good).

Morels can also be canned. Clean and split. Steam for four minutes or heat in a saucepan for fifteen minutes. Pack hot mushrooms to within one-half inch of the tops of canning jars. Add boiling cooking liquid or hot water. Adjust pint or half-pint jar lids. Process in a pressure canner, at ten pounds of pressure, for thirty minutes.

> *MOVIE "Attack of the Mushroom People" 2 stars. (1966) Akira Kubo, Niki Yashiro. Shipwreck survivor meets munchies. (Actual TV Guide listing).*

The Bohemian word for "morels" is "hobies".

II.

Basic Recipes

There are many ways to prepare morel mushrooms for the table, some of the most delectable and popular are also the simplest. It would be hard to top morels either sautéed in hot butter for three to five minutes, or fried in bacon grease six to eight minutes. The rich, delicate meaty flavor is brought out both ways. They also are first steps in many delightful recipes.

Many people never get beyond basic morel cookery, and with good reason. Scramble morels with eggs for breakfast. Chop them and add them to gravy. Use them to make a meaty sauce and serve atop a steak. Cook them into spaghetti sauce. Put them in omelets and in mushroom soup. Ground dried morels to use as a seasoning powder. Cook them in a marinade. Chop them and include them in meat loaf. Batter and deep fry them. Stuff them with cooked meat (chicken, veal, ham), roll in bread crumbs, season and broil. Use your imagination. There's no limit to using morels as a main dish, side dish, in sauces and soups, as a seasoning, with vegetables and meats. If you do run out of ideas, here's a few more...

*The American Food and Wine Festival, held annu-
ally in San Francisco, California, is highlighted by
the arrival of one hundred pounds of fresh morels, flown
in with the Michigan delegation.*

Violet

BASIC BACON & MORELS

Use any amount of morels and one-fourth as much bacon. This is
great itself (my personal favorite)as an appetizer, over a steak or in a grilled
cheese sandwich — easy and fast to prepare in the field or at home.

This will sound a little crazy, but follow this method...Cut bacon into
small pieces. Fry at high heat until ready to remove and drain, but leave in
pan. Do not turn heat down. (Bacon will not get any crisper after morels
are added due to the morel's moisture content--this is the secret). Do not
remove grease. Add clean, split morels. Liquid will become "soupy". Cook
until liquid is clear. Mixture will make a light "popping" noise. Drain. Eat
or use in an omelet or quiche, or in a sandwich. The bacon gives the morels
a bit of a smoky flavor and the morels give the bacon a meaty flavor--a very
good way to extend that delicious morel taste.

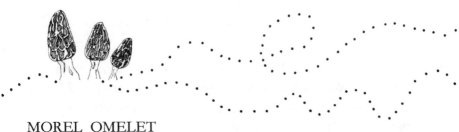

MOREL OMELET

Simmer morels in a little butter and their own juices until liquid has evaporated. Then add to omelet mixture and cook as usual.

This is another example of what I feel is the best way to use morels in cooking: simply. Generally prepare morels separately, then add to recipe. Morels tend to absorb some of the flavor of other ingredients (such as onion or green pepper) and could disguise some of the unique meaty taste of the morels.

Morel heaven.

MOREL BUTTER

Yield: 1/2 pound

1/4 pound fresh morels
2 tablespoons butter
1/4 pound butter (room temperature)
1 teaspoon chives, chopped

Finely chop morels by hand or in food processor. Melt 2 tablespoons butter in large skillet; add morels and sauté for 5 minutes. Cool thoroughly.
Whip butter to make it fluffy. Blend in cooled morels and chives.
Use as a spread or add to cooked vegetables or baked potatoes. Keeps well in refrigerator for a week in tightly covered container.

Mushroom "Kits". I've personally purchased and tried at least two of every kit I've found on the market. Most are simply germinated spore in a growing medium. Some require complicated mixtures of gardening soils and materials. All have the buyer looking for results in the regular Spring morel season or the following year. Unfortunately the products tend to be inconsistent and the success rate poor. There have been some exceptions over the years, but what actually DID work is generally not available. You CAN, however, "seed" areas to improve your chances – and at no expense! Simply use a mesh bag while collecting. As you walk gently lift the bottom

of the bag and let it back down. This will increase the opportunities for spore to drop. You can also introduce spore to woods and fields that never had morels before by taking a mesh bag of morels you picked elsewhere and strolling through areas you'd like to find morels in the future. Of course, the pH and other factors need to be correct for morels to flourish, but the chances of this working I believe are better than any kit: more spore, more variety of spore, exposure to more area. I've done this with great success (actually created some of my best hunting spots). But it takes time for the whole process to work. It works best when it becomes a habit.

may you find
what you seek

My Christmas card one year.

III.

Main Dishes

BUFFET MORNAY

Yield: 6 servings
1 pound morels
1 can crabmeat (6-1/2 to 7-3/4 ounces)
2 teaspoons lemon juice
3 tablespoons butter
3 tablespoons all-purpose flour
1-1/2 cups shredded processed cheese
2 tablespoons sherry

Preheat oven to 350 degrees. Split morels. Arrange the halves, hollow side up, in an 8-inch baking dish. Cover with flaked crabmeat. Sprinkle with lemon juice. Melt butter. Blend in flour. Add 1-1/2 cups milk, all at once. Cook and stir until thickened. Add small amount of this mixture to egg yolks. Return to sauce. Cook one minute. Remove from heat. Stir in 1-1/4 cups cheese and sherry. Pour over crab. Sprinkle with 1/4 cup cheese. Bake 20 minutes, till hot. Serve over rice or toast.

CHICKEN & MOREL CUTLETS

Yield: 4 to 6 servings

1/4 pound morels, finely chopped
18 tablespoons (9 ounces) butter
1-1/2 pounds boned raw chicken
2 cups breadcrumbs
1/3 cup light cream
3 tablespoons parsley, chopped
1 egg, beaten Salt
Pepper

Cook mushrooms in one ounce of butter for 10 minutes at medium heat. Set aside to cool. Soak 2/3 of the breadcrumbs in the cream. Add to the chicken and mince, or put through a meat grinder. Cream 4 ounces of the butter to soften it. Mix in the meat, mushrooms and parsley. Season to taste with salt and pepper.

With wet fingers (keep a bowl of water handy) form the mixture into oval cakes about 1/2-inch thick. There should be enough for about 16 to 18. Turn them in beaten egg and then in the remaining breadcrumbs. Refrigerate.

Clarify the remaining butter by first bringing to a boil, then straining through a muslin-lined sieve. Put half the clarified butter into a large frying pan. Cook the cutlets gently on both sides until they are crisp and golden brown on the outside and soft, but cooked through, inside, about 15 to 20 minutes. Place on a serving dish and pour the remaining clarified butter over them.

These cutlets can be prepared a day or two in advance. Store them in the refrigerator.

From the dawn of civilization, in Talmud and Chaldean writings, mushrooms were mentioned as food.

A freshly "popped" black morel. Though often difficult to spot, morels are truly beautiful natural masterpieces to behold — like snowflakes, each one unique, each a treasure.

*Some people feel that mushrooms are the primal sym-
bol of the lunar force that is in all of us, our night side
expressed by dreams, trances and altered consciousness.*

*In Europe, where the morel is a long-recognized
delicacy, people once routinely set fire to woods to
stimulate a good crop of morels the following Spring.*

CREAMED FISH WITH MORELS

Yield: 4 servings

5 tablespoon butter, divided
3 tablespoons flour
2 cups milk
1 tablespoons lemon juice
1-1/2 cups cooked fish
Salt
Freshly ground pepper
1 tablespoon parsley, minced
1/2 pound morels, sliced

Sauté morels in 2 tablespoons butter five minutes. Set aside. Heat remaining butter in a heavy-bottomed saucepan. Stir in flour and cook until
smooth, about two minutes. Slowly add milk, continuing to stir. Add morels. Simmer for two minutes. Mix the lemon juice into the fish and add to
the cream sauce. Salt and pepper to taste. Heat thoroughly. Remove from
heat and sprinkle with parsley. Serve over toast or rice.

FILLET OF BEEF WITH MORELS

Yield: 4 servings
1 pound onions, sliced
Milk
Flour
Deep fat for frying 4 tenderloin steaks
2 tablespoons freshly ground black pepper
12 tablespoons butter
2 tablespoons herbs, finely ground
  (tarragon, parsley, marjoram, chives, basil, chervil, as available)
1/3 cup dry sherry
1/2 pound morels
1 tablespoon cornstarch
1/3 cup beef stock
Salt
Pepper

Dip the onions in milk and drain. Put them into a paper bag with a couple of tablespoons of flour and shake, coating. Deep fry them. Keep warm in oven.

Rub the steaks with the pepper. Sauté them in half the butter, about 3 minutes a side. Remove and keep warm. Add the remaining butter, herbs and sherry to the steak pan. Add mushrooms and cook five minutes. Mix the cornstarch with the beef stock and add to the sauce. Season with salt and pepper, to taste, as sauce slightly thickens.

Arrange the steaks on a serving dish. Pour the mushroom sauce over them and put onion rings around the edge of the dish.

These white morels are very similar in size and shape but the locations are quite different. The top one was found deep in hardwoods. The other on a cemetery lawn. Predictability is often not the strong suit of the morel.

FISH WITH CREAM AND MORELS

Yield: 4 servings
4 whole fish (trout, whiting, etc.) or 4 thick fillets
           (halibut, sole, flounder)
Seasoned flour
6 tablespoons butter
1/2 pound morels, sliced
 Salt
Pepper
Lemon juice
2 cups heavy cream
Cayenne pepper (pinch)

    Turn the fish in seasoned flour. Clarify the butter: bring it to a boil in a small pan then pour it through a muslin-lined sieve into a frying pan. Brown the fish on both sides over high heat in the butter. Transfer fish to a dish and cook the morels in the fish juices. Season to taste with salt and pepper. Sprinkle with lemon juice and return fish to pan. Pour the cream over the fish, add a pinch of cayenne pepper, and bring to a boil. When the cream is bubbling gently, place the dish under a hot grill for about 8 minutes until a golden crusty skin forms on top. Do not overcook. Serve hot in cooking dish.

HOPE BAY TROUT STUFFED WITH MORELS

Yield: 6 servings

6 Trout, small, heads on
1 package dry stuffing mix
8 tablespoons butter, divided
1 pound morels, sliced
1 tablespoon fresh parsley, chopped
Salt
Pepper

Prepare dry stuffing mix as directed on package.
Sauté morels in 4 tablespoons of butter for ten minutes.
Mix with stuffing. Add parsley.
Pre-heat oven to 350 degrees. Wash trout in cold water. Pat dry. Lightly salt and pepper cavity. Stuff with mixture.

Place trout side by side in shallow, buttered baking dish, melt remainder of butter and pour over fish. Add one tablespoon of water and bake for 15 minutes. Baste with more melted butter and bake another 10 to 15 minutes. To see if they are done, stick a fork in the thickest part just behind the head. The meat should flake to the bone. (Suggestion: serve with boiled new potatoes and cooked asparagus, both in abundance during morel season.)

In some earlier times, mushroom eating was synonymous with the undisciplined love of luxuries.

MORELS WITH HAM

Yield: 4 servings

1/2 pound fresh morels
2 pounds ham, thickly sliced
1-1/2 cups beef broth
3/4 cup semi-sweet white wine
1 egg yolk, beaten
1/2 cup cream
1 pinch salt
1 pinch pepper

Place ham slices in a well-greased (buttered) casserole dish. Pour in beef broth and wine. Simmer 1-1/2 to 2 hours. When ham is well-cooked, place it in deep serving dish and keep warm. Sauté morels in butter in a large frying pan. Add one cup of liquid from the ham. Stirring constantly, add egg yolk and cream. When thick, add salt and pepper. Pour over ham and serve.

MOREL QUICHE

Yield: 4-6 servings

1 pound morels
1/4 pound bacon
1/2 cup chopped onion
1/2 cup chopped green pepper
1-1/2 cups shredded baby Swiss cheese
1-1/2 cups milk
3/4 cup Bisquick
3 eggs
1 teaspoon salt
1/4 teaspoon pepper

Prepare BASIC BACON & MOREL mixture (see index).

Preheat oven to 400 degrees. In a 10-inch lightly greased pie pan mix bacon & mushrooms, onion, green pepper and cheese. In medium-sized bowl add milk, Bisquick, eggs, salt and pepper. Beat until smooth. Pour into pie pan. Bake 35-40 minutes or until inserted toothpick comes out clean.

There are old mushroom hunters
And there are bold mushroom hunters
But there are no bold old mushroom hunters.

MOREL MEAT LOAF

Yield: 6 servings

1 pound ground beef
1/2 pound morels
1 cup dry breadcrumbs or cracker crumbs
1-1/4 cups milk
1 egg
1 small onion, chopped (about 1/4 cup)
1 tablespoon Worcestershire sauce
1-1/2 teaspoons salt
1/2 teaspoon dry mustard
1/4 teaspoon pepper
1/4 teaspoon ground sage
1 clove garlic, crushed (optional)
2 tablespoons butter.

Sauté morels in butter, medium heat for three minutes. Mix with all other ingredients in large bowl. Spread in ungreased loaf pan 9 x 5 x 3 inches. Cook uncovered in oven at 350 degrees until done, about 1-1/2 hours. Serve with MUSHROOM GRAVY (see INDEX).

"Life could go on very nicely without people, but not without fungi."

Early in America, mushrooms were a luxury for those who could afford to dine lavishly.

MOREL PILAF

Yield: 4 servings

3 tablespoons olive oil
3 tablespoons onion, fine
1 cup long-grain rice
1/2 teaspoon salt
1/4 teaspoon freshly ground pepper
2 cups beef broth
1/2 pound morels
2 tablespoons butter

Sauté morels in butter for five minutes. Set aside. Heat olive oil in saucepan. Add onion and cook, stirring often, until soft. Add rice and cook over low heat, stirring constantly, for three minutes. Add salt, pepper, beef broth and mushrooms. Cover and simmer 20 minutes or transfer to a covered casserole and bake at 350 degrees for one hour.

MOREL-STUFFED CHICKEN BREASTS

Yield: 4 to 6 servings

1/4 pound plus 4 tablespoons butter
1/2 pound morels, finely chopped
1/2 teaspoon salt
1/4 teaspoon freshly ground pepper
1-1/2 cups freshly made bread crumbs
1/4 teaspoon nutmeg
4 chicken breasts, skinned and halved
1 cup heavy cream

Preheat over to 350 degrees. Melt 1/4 pound butter in a skillet. Add morels, salt and pepper and cook, stirring often, until mushrooms absorb most of the butter. Remove from heat and stir in 3/4 cup of bread crumbs and the nutmeg. Divide the mushroom stuffing into 8 portions and place a portion in the center of each piece of chicken. Fold the chicken around the stuffing and place, seam side down, in a shallow casserole dish. Melt the remaining 4 tablespoons of butter and brush over chicken. Sprinkle with the remaining 3/4 cup of bread crumbs. Pour on the cream and bake for 30 minutes until lightly brown.

PAN CHICKEN & MORELS

Yield: 6 servings

3 pounds chicken pieces Seasoned flour
4 tablespoons butter
2 tablespoons oil
1/3   cup dry white wine
1-1/2 pounds morels, cleaned, sliced
4 cups heavy cream
1 large egg yolk
Salt
Freshly ground black pepper
Lemon juice (optional)

Turn the chicken in seasoned flour and color lightly in the butter and oil. Pour in wine and cook briskly until it has almost evaporated, turning the chicken pieces in the juices. Add morels and cream and cook, uncovered, until chicken is done. Remove it, and as many morels as possible, to a hot serving dish. Boil down the sauce by about half. Thicken the sauce further by beating the egg yolk with a little of the sauce then cooking it all together, just below the boiling point, for about 5 minutes. Season to taste with salt and pepper. Lemon juice may be added (if desired). Pour over chicken and serve. Boiled and buttered rice goes well with this dish.

Our word "morel" comes from the French "morille"

RISSOTO

Yield: 6-8 portions

4 large onions, finely chopped
6 tablespoons bacon grease
1 pound cubed veal (or beef)
1 pound cubed pork
1 tablespoon salt
1/3 cup canned tomatoes (and juice)
4 ounces fresh morels
3/4 cup rice, well washed
1 cup canned peas (and juice)
1 cup broth (or use bouillon cube dissolved in 1-1/2 cups water)

Brown onions in fat. Add the cubed meat and brown twenty minutes. Add salt and tomatoes; simmer for twenty minutes. Add morels. Simmer for ten minutes. Stir frequently to this point. Add rice and peas with juice, spreading evenly. <u>Do not stir</u> after rice is added, but shake the pan gently several times. Cover tightly and cook over low heat, adding a cup of broth to the rice as it cooks so the mixture remains moist. If more broth is needed, add a little at a time. Simmer 15 to 20 minutes until rice puffs and is done. The finished dish should be moist, not dry or too wet. Stir before serving. At table grated Parmesan cheese may be sprinkled over top.

ROAST CHICKEN & MORELS

Yield: 4 servings

1 large roasting chicken
1-1/2 cups morels (sliced lengthwise)
2 tablespoons chicken drippings
2 tablespoons butter
Salt
2 tablespoons flour
1 teaspoon lemon juice
1 teaspoon chopped fresh parsley
1-1/2 cups heavy cream

Roast chicken until golden brown and done. Split into four equal pieces on a platter. Keep warm. In a large frying pan, sauté morels in drippings and butter over low heat for five minutes. Sprinkle with salt and push morels to side of pan. Stir in flour until smooth, then mix together with morels and continue to cook another two minutes. Stir in cream until it thickens. Add lemon juice and parsley. Pour over chicken and serve immediately. Also delicious served over toast.

SPAGHETTI WITH CHICKEN & MORELS

Yield: 6 servings

1 3-pound chicken, disjointed
1/2 cup butter
1 teaspoon salt
1/2 cup chopped celery leaves
1 small onion, chopped
1 cup boiling water
1 pound morels, thickly sliced
3 tablespoons flour
Heavy cream
2/3 cup grated Romano cheese
1/4 cup dry sherry
 1 pound spaghetti, cooked according to package directions

Brown chicken in three tablespoons of butter. Add salt, celery, onion and water. Cover. Simmer until chicken is tender, about 30 minutes. Cool. Remove bones and cube meat.

Sauté morels in two tablespoons of butter minutes at medium heat. Add the chicken.

Melt the remaining three tablespoons of butter in a saucepan. Add flour and stir with a wire whisk until blended. Meanwhile, to the chicken broth add enough cream to make three cups of liquid. Bring to a boil and add all at once to the butter-flour mixture, stirring vigorously with the whisk. Stir in the cheese and add the chicken and mushrooms. Stir in the sherry and heat but do not boil. Correct the seasonings. Serve over hot spaghetti.

VEAL WITH MORELS

Yield: 4 servings

1 cup fresh morels (1/3 oz. dried)
1/3 cup morel liquid (see directions)
8 slices veal scallops (about 1-1/2 pounds)
Salt and freshly ground pepper (to taste)
Flour, for coating
4 tablespoons butter
4 cups finely chopped onion
1/2 cup whipping cream
1/2 cup milk
1 tablespoon flour
1 teaspoon lemon juice
1/8 teaspoon cayenne pepper

Soak morels well in advance if dried morels are used. Set aside. If fresh are used, cover with water and simmer gently for three minutes. Save the liquid.

Pound veal lightly with flat mallet. Sprinkle with salt and pepper and coat lightly in flour. Shake off excess. Heat 3 tablespoons butter in heavy skillet (medium heat) and add veal pieces. Cook 5-6 minutes, turning once to brown well on both sides.

Remove veal to a warm platter. Add onion to skillet and briefly sauté. Add morels and morel liquid. Cook until liquid is reduced by half. Add cream and milk and bring to simmer (low heat). Blend one tablespoon butter and flour well and add gradually, stirring into liquid. When thickened and smooth, add salt and pepper, lemon juice and cayenne. Pour sauce over veal.

IV.

Appetizers & Side Dishes

BAKED NUT & VEGETABLE STUFFED MORELS

Yield: about 15 mushrooms

12 ounces fresh morels
2 tablespoons butter or margarine
1/3 cup diced celery
2 tablespoons chopped onion
1 small garlic clove, crushed
1/2 cup soft bread crumbs
2 tablespoons chopped walnuts
1/4 teaspoon salt
Ground black pepper (pinch)
1 teaspoon lemon juice

Preheat oven to 400 degrees. Clean and dry mushrooms. Remove stems. Chop stems and set aside (about 3/4 cup). Place mushrooms, cavity side down, on lightly greased baking sheet. Bake until partly cooked, about four minutes. Remove from oven. Set aside. In large skillet melt butter. Add celery, onion, garlic and reserved chopped stems. Sauté until tender, about five minutes. Remove from heat. Stir in bread crumbs, walnuts, salt, pepper and lemon juice. Spoon into mushroom caps. Bake until mixture is golden, about five minutes.

BAKED TOMATOES WITH MOREL STUFFING

Yield: 4 servings

4 firm large tomatoes
Salt
1/2 cup dried homemade bread crumbs
2 tablespoons onion, finely chopped
Coarsely ground pepper
1/2 pound morels, chopped
4 tablespoons butter

Preheat over to 400 degrees. Film a shallow baking pan with oil using a pan large enough so 8 tomato halves will not be crowded. Carefully cut a slice from the top of each tomato and scoop out most of the pulp, leaving a thick shell so tomatoes will hold their shape. Sprinkle the insides of tomato shells with salt, invert them on paper towels. Let them drain for about 15 minutes. Squeeze the juice out of the pulp and finely chop pulp. Set aside.

In a frying pan melt 4 tablespoons butter. Add mushrooms and sauté three minutes at medium-high heat. Push mushrooms toward handle of pan and tilt pan so remaining butter is free of mushrooms and on burner. Add onion and sauté one minute. Allow to cool.

In a bowl lightly toss bread crumbs, tomato pulp, mushrooms and onion, salt and pepper. Lightly fill each tomato, without packing. Place on a baking pan and bake 15 to 20 minutes.

On March 12, 1984 a law was passed by Minnesota Legislature designating <u>Morchella esculenta</u>, or white morel, the official State Mushroom.

BLEU CHEESED MORELS

Yield: 4 to 6 servings

12 to 14 large morels
1/4 cup green onions, chopped
1/4 cup butter or margarine
1/4 cup (one ounce) bleu cheese, crumbled
1/3 cup fine dry breadcrumbs Salt (to taste) Pepper (to taste)

Preheat oven to 350 degrees. Remove stems from morels. Chop stems. Cook stems and onion in butter until tender but not brown. Add cheese, 2 tablespoons of crumbs, salt and pepper. Fill morel caps with mixture. Sprinkle with remaining crumbs. Place on baking sheet. Bake for 12 minutes.

BROILED MOREL CAPS

Yield: 3 servings

2 tablespoons fine bread crumbs
1 tablespoon parsley, chopped
1/4 clove garlic, minced
12 morels, caps only
2 tablespoons cooking oil
Salt (to taste)
Freshly ground pepper (to taste)

Mix together crumbs, parsley and garlic., Brush mushroom caps with oil and roll in crumbs. Sprinkle with salt and pepper. Broil mushrooms under moderate heat, about five minutes on each side. Sprinkle with more oil, if necessary. Serve as a garnish for meats.

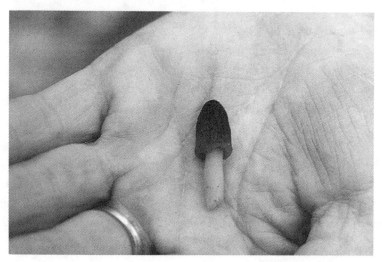

A tiny black morel. They're especially difficult to spot when they're this size.

Top quality dried morels sell for $15.00 – $17.00 an ounce, or $240 - $272 a pound. One dried pound is equal to eight pounds of fresh.

CAULIFLOWER MORELS AU GRATIN

Yield: 4 servings

1 large cauliflower
1/2 pound morels, chopped
1 cup milk
6 tablespoons flour
1/3 cup butter
1/2 cup cheese, grated
3 tablespoons breadcrumbs
Chopped parsley

Soak cauliflower in cold water for 15 minutes. Remove and boil in salted water until just soft. Remove and divide into flowerlets. Simmer morels in milk until tender, about 10 minutes. Blend in flour and half the butter. Add milk gradually, season and cook until smooth. Pour into shallow dish. Arrange cauliflower on top. Sprinkle cheese and crumbs on top. Melt remaining butter. Lightly broil until brown. Garnish with parsley.

CREAMED MORELS

Yield: 6 servings

1-1/2 pounds morels
6 ounces butter
3 tablespoons flour
1-1/2 pints cream (or milk)
Salt (to taste)
Pepper (to taste)

Cut morels into small pieces. Heat butter. When it begins to smoke, drop mushrooms in and cover. Cook 10 minutes, stirring occasionally. Remove cover, draw morels to one side. Tilt pan so that juice runs to the other side. Into this work the flour and when smooth, add cream (or milk). Stir the mushrooms into this and allow to boil one minute. Season taste. (Can also be served on toast or pre-prepared pastry shells.)

CREAMED MUSHROOM PUFFS

Yield: about 16 puffs
Pastry
1/4 cup butter
2/3 cup water
1 teaspoon sugar
1 cup flour
4 eggs
Filling
1 1/2 pounds mushrooms, halved
6 tablespoons butter, divided
1/3 cup white wine
lemon juice (one lemon)
2 cups half and half cream
Salt (to taste)
Ground Pepper (to taste)
2 tablespoons arrowroot or flour
1/4 cup brandy

In medium saucepan, heat butter, water and sugar until boiling. Remove from heat. Add flour and beat until well mixed. Set over heat again and cook three minutes or until the mixture leaves the sides of the pan. Cool five minutes. Beat in eggs, one at a time. Drop dough by tablespoons on a baking sheet, leaving space between each. Bake in 400 degree oven for 10 minutes. Reduce heat to 350 degrees and bake until firm to the touch, about 20 more minutes. Cool on wire rack.

For filling, cook mushrooms in medium saucepan with three tablespoons of butter for four minutes. Add wine and lemon juice. Pour in cream. Bring to a boil and cook until reduced, about five minutes. Season with salt and pepper. Dissolve arrowroot or flour in brandy and add to sauce. Cook and stir sauce until smooth and thickened. Remove from heat and quickly add remaining three tablespoons of butter.

Slice puffs horizontally. Remove any excess dough on inside and fill with mushroom mixture.

CUCUMBER STUFFED WITH MORELS & BEEF

Yield: 4 servings

1 large cucumber
1 ounce butter (or drippings)
1/2 pound morels
1/2 pound beef, minced
Salt
Pepper
Drippings (or butter) for basting

Skin the cucumber and cut into 3-inch lengths. Cut lengthwise through each piece. Remove center and chop finely. Heat butter and lightly sauté morels. Stir in meat, then the cucumber pulp. Season well. Put the cucumber "boats" into boiling salted water and cook 5 minutes only. Drain carefully and fill with mushroom/meat mixture. Lightly grease small baking tin, place cucumber boats inside. Bake in middle of oven for 35 to 40 minutes at 375 degrees. Baste from time to time (Suggestion: with MOREL SAUCE, see INDEX)

DEVILED MORELS

Yield: 4-6 servings

2   cups morels
1   cup bread crumbs
2   hard-boiled egg yolks
2   raw egg yolks
1   cup milk (or cream)
4   tablespoons butter
Salt
Pepper

Chop morels. Mix the mashed yolks of the hard-boiled eggs with the raw ones in a mixing bowl and stir in milk or cream. On the bottom of a baking pan or dish put a layer of bread crumbs, then a layer of mushrooms. Scatter bits of butter on. Pour on egg and cream mixture, saving enough for a top layer of bread crumbs and butter. Add that top layer. Bake for 20 minutes, closely covered, in a hot oven. Uncover and bake for five more minutes, or long enough for the top to be well-browned.

Another common belief is that touching a poison-ous mushroom can kill a person. In reality, any poison is contained inside the cap and stalk.

A man from New York flew into Traverse City, Michigan, rented a chauffeur and a Limousine, drove 30 miles to Mesick (one of several Michigan cities that claim to be the Mushroom Capitol of the World), bought every morel he could find, and returned to New York.

DILL - HERBED MORELS

Yield: 3 or 4 servings

1/2 pound morels
2 tablespoons butter or margarine
1 cup sour cream
1 teaspoon dill seed
1/4 teaspoon salt
Paprika
Freshly ground pepper (dash)
Nutmeg (dash)
Hot toast points

Split morels. Melt butter in skillet. Add mushrooms and cover. Cook, stirring occasionally, over medium heat about 8 minutes. Stir in sour cream and seasonings. Reduce heat. Cook and stir (over low heat) until just heated through. Dash with paprika. Serve over toast points.

MORELS WITH CHEESE FILLING

Yield: 4 servings

1 egg yolk
1/2 pound morels
2 ounces milk
1 tablespoon onion, fried
4 rashers bacon, chopped and fried
1 tablespoons fresh breadcrumbs
2 ounces Cheddar or Parmesan cheese,
Salt (finely grated) and Pepper
8 slices tomato (thick), lightly fried
1 teaspoon parsley, finely chopped

Clean and split morels. Remove and chop stems. Add all to milk and lightly poach. Remove and drain. Mix together the fried onion, fried bacon, breadcrumbs, cheese and seasonings (to taste). Blend in egg yolk then spoon the mixture into the open sides of the morels. Broil for 3 to 5 minutes then place on fried tomato slices. Transfer to serving dish and sprinkle with parsley.

The Latin "mussiriones" is the first recorded mention of the fungus we call mushrooms

Our word "mushroom" comes from the French "mousseron".

MORELS ELEGANTE

Yield: 6 servings
1/2 pound morels
3 tablespoons butter or margarine
2 tablespoons onion, minced
1 tablespoon all-purpose flour
 Salt (dash)
Pepper (dash)
1 cup light cream
2 tablespoons Parmesan cheese
1 tablespoon lemon juice
2 egg yolks, slightly beaten
1 teaspoon butter, melted
1 tablespoon dry breadcrumbs

Clean morels. Slice thin. Melt butter in skillet. Sauté mushrooms, then onion, keeping initially separate. Mix together. Sprinkle with flour and toss to coat. Season with salt and pepper. Cook over low heat until tender, about 15 minutes. Stir in cream, Parmesan cheese and lemon juice. Heat through.

Add small amount of hot cream mixture to egg yolks. Mix and return to cream mixture. Cook and stir one minute longer. Serve in sauce dishes. (suggested garnish - 1 teaspoon melted butter mixed with breadcrumbs).

Commercial mushroom growing in the United States began about the time of the Civil War, from imported spawn, on Long Island in New York.

Proper clothing is important. Long-sleeved shirts and long pants will shield against briars, brambles, poison ivy and insects. Comfortable, waterproof boots or walking shoes are a necessity. Carrying a stick or cane can be of use to combat aggressive bushes, in testing the passability of swampy areas and in moving grass and leaves while you're searching.

MORELS MING TOY

Yield: 4 servings

1/2 pound morels
1 tablespoon all-purpose flour
3 tablespoons butter or margarine
1/2 teaspoon soy sauce
Salt (dash)
Pepper (dash)

Split morels in half. Rinse. Sprinkle lightly with flour. Melt butter in pan. Add soy sauce. When mixed, add mushrooms. Cook, covered, over low heat 8 to 10 minutes, turning occasionally. Season.

MORELS NORMANDIE
Yield: 6 servings

2 pounds morels
3/4 cup butter
1 cup heavy cream (or cream and sour cream mixed)
2 tomatoes, peeled, chopped, seeded
Salt (to taste)
Pepper (to taste)
6 slices bread, fried in butter

Split larger morels in half. Place in saucepan and cover with cold water. Bring to a boil and cook two minutes. Drain. In medium saucepan melt butter. Add morels and cook five minutes. Add cream. Press excess liquid from tomatoes. Add to mushroom mixture. Season to taste with salt and pepper. Simmer until sauce is thickened, about ten minutes. Pour into deep serving dish and line edges with fried bread slices.

Superstitions from the past had mushrooms attributed to thunder and fairies.

MOREL TURNOVERS

Yield: about 24 turnovers

3   3-ounce packages cream cheese, at room temperature
1/2 cup butter, at room temperature
1-1/2 cups flour

Mushroom Filling

3 tablespoons butter
1 large onion, finely chopped
1/2 pound morels, finely chopped
1/4 teaspoon thyme
1/2 teaspoon salt
Freshly ground pepper (to taste)
2 tablespoons flour
1/4 cup sweet or sour cream

Mix cream cheese and butter thoroughly. Add flour and work with fingers or pastry blender until smooth. Chill well, for at least 30 minutes. Preheat oven to 450 degrees. Roll dough to 1/8 inch thickness on a lightly floured surface and cut into rounds with a three-inch biscuit cutter. Place a teaspoon of mushroom filling on each and fold the dough over the filling. Press the edges together with a fork. Prick top crusts to allow for the escape of steam. Place on an ungreased baking sheet and bake until lightly browned, about 15 minutes.

Filling

In a skillet, heat the butter, add the onion and brown lightly. Add the mushrooms and cook, stirring often, about three minutes. Add thyme, salt and pepper, and sprinkle with flour. Stir in the cream and cook gently until thickened.

Welcome to the

Boyne City, Michigan

There are many local, regional, national and international mushroom festivals -- great sources of fun, information and (usually) mushrooms.

The Second Annual
ILLINOIS STATE
MOREL MUSHROOM
HUNTING CHAMPIONSHIP
SATURDAY, MAY 3, 1997 • MAGNOLIA, ILLINOIS

*This wasn't a competition.
This was a celebration.
John Husar, Chicago Tribune*

In the fanatic morel tradition the www.morelheaven. com website sells caps, carved mushrooms, walking sticks, jewelry, T-shirts, books, videos, posters & more— all part of the fun of the "morel experience". Check online or call 1-877-667-3518 for a free product catalog.

MOREL ZUCCHINI EGG BAKE

Yield: 2 servings

8 ounces fresh morels
2 tablespoons vegetable oil
2/3 cup chopped onion
1 cup zucchini, cut in half lengthwise and sliced 1/4-inch thick
6 eggs
1-1/2 teaspoon salt
1 teaspoon Italian seasoning
Ground black pepper (pinch)
1/2 cup shredded cheddar cheese

Preheat oven to 350 degrees Clean and split morels (about 2-3/4 cups). In large skillet, heat til until hot. Add onion and mushrooms. Sauté about two minutes. Shake pan occasionally. Add zucchini. Sauté until zucchini is crisp/tender and other vegetables are tender, about three minutes. Remove from heat. In medium bowl beat together eggs, salt, Italian seasoning and black pepper. Reserve a few morels for later use and add remaining morel/vegetable mixture to eggs. Pour into two greased shallow 16-ounce casseroles. Bake, uncovered, until mixture is almost firm, about ten minutes. Sprinkle with cheese and top with reserved morels. Increase oven heat to 450 degrees. Bake, uncovered, until cheese is melted and mushrooms are hot, about ten minutes.

In the courts of France and the castles of Britain, mushrooms were a delicacy for royalty and the very rich.

It was a common belief that poisonous mushrooms would turn a silver spoon black. In fact, many edible mushrooms will do the same.

MUSHROOM TOAST

Yield: 4 servings

1 large shallot, minced
4 tablespoons butter, divided
1/2 cup chopped (black forest) ham
1/4 pound morels, cut into strips
2 tablespoons vermouth
1 egg yolk
1/2 cup heavy (or whipping) cream
1 teaspoon lemon juice
1 pinch crushed, dried hot red peppers
2 tablespoons chopped fresh parsley
4 slices hot buttered toast (preferably homemade)

In a large heavy skillet sauté shallots in 2 tablespoons butter until soft. Add ham. Cook 4 minutes over medium-low heat. Add remaining butter and morels. Raise heat slightly and cook one minute, tossing mushrooms to coat evenly with mixture. Sprinkle with vermouth. Cook one minute longer. Reduce heat to low.

In small bowl combine egg yolk and cream. Stir into mushroom mixture. Add lemon juice and peppers.

Cook over low heat until thickened. Do not boil. Garnish with parsley. Serve over buttered toast.

PEA & ONION STUFFED MORELS

Yield: about 20 mushrooms

1 pound morels (about 20)
1 10-ounce package frozen peas
6 small green onions, chopped finely
4 tablespoons margarine
1 pinch garlic powder
Salt (to taste)
Pepper (to taste)
1 tablespoon soy sauce

Clean and cut morels in two. Remove morel stems and chop finely. Mix with frozen peas and onions. Add margarine, garlic, salt, pepper and soy sauce.

Stuff morel heads with mixture and place on greased baking sheet. Cover with aluminum foil. Bake at 450 degrees for 35 to 40 minutes.

Ancient Greeks and Romans believed mushrooms where formed where lightning struck.

PECAN - STUFFED MORELS

Yield: 8 servings
1 pound morels
1/2 cup butter
1 cup chopped onion
1 cup chopped celery
1 teaspoon salt
1/2 teaspoon black pepper
1/2 teaspoon paprika
5 cups dry bread crumbs
1-1/2 cups pecans, coarsely chopped
Beaten eggs
Melted butter

Clean morels, trim off stems, set stems aside.

Melt butter in large heavy skillet and sauté onion, celery and chopped morel stems until tender and transparent. Stir in seasonings, bread crumbs and pecans. Stir in enough beaten eggs to moisten mixture. Put filling in pastry bag and stuff morels. Set stuffed morels, points up, on a buttered baking sheet. Drizzle with melted butter and bake at 350 degrees for 20 to 30 minutes. Serve upright on chopped parsley or other greens.

FEE....$12.50   No. 3124834008
RESIDENT MUSHROOM LICENSE
Name *Larry "Tree" Lonik*
is hereby authorized to hunt, pick, pluck, snatch,
grab, shuck, shell, thresh, combine, string, gather,
husk, hoist, harvest, chop, grub, gig, shoot, spear,
lance, stab, or otherwise latch onto mushroomus
fungi of edible specie. Use of trot lines, trammel nets,
bulldozers, chain saws, and TNT strictly forbidden!

                                        Issuing Officer

POTATOES GRATIN WITH MUSHROOMS

Yield: 4 servings

1 pound potatoes
1/2 pound morels Butter
1 clove garlic, finely chopped
Salt
Pepper
2/3 cup light cream
2/3 cup heavy cream
1/4 cup water
4 tablespoons grated Parmesan or hard Cheddar cheese

Peel the potatoes (if desired) and slice thinly. Slice mushrooms. Grease an oval shallow gratin dish generously with butter and sprinkle garlic over it. Arrange half the potatoes, slices overlapping, on the bottom of the dish. Salt and pepper to taste and put in the morels. Lightly season again and finish off with a final layer of potatoes. Mix the cream and the water and pour over. Sprinkle cheese on top. Dot with butter. Bake for 1-1/2 hours at 325 pre-heated degrees. The top of the dish will turn a crisp-looking golden brown with the cream bubbling up around the edges.

POTATO & WILD MUSHROOM GRATIN

Yield: 6 servings

1-1/2 pounds new red potatoes
1/2 pound morels
4 tablespoons unsalted butter
3 tablespoons heavy cream
1/2 teaspoon minced garlic
Salt (to taste)
Pepper (to taste)

Peel potatoes and slice them 1/4-inch thick. Put in cold water for 30 minutes, changing water every 10 minutes. Clean and coarsely chop morels. Set in 1-1/4 cups warm water 10 minutes. Strain morels, but save liquid. Sauté mushrooms in two tablespoons butter 5 to 6 minutes. Halfway through cooking, stir in heavy cream, garlic, salt and pepper.

Towel potatoes dry. In a lightly buttered casserole dish arrange them in a layer. Salt potatoes lightly and spoon some of the mushroom mixture over them. Continue layering, ending with potatoes. Dot potatoes with butter and bake in a pre-heated 425 degree oven for 15 to 20 minutes or until potatoes are tender and deep golden brown.

Governor Rudy Perpich signs the bill making the morel (<u>Morchella esculenta</u>) Minnesota's official state mushroom. House author Phyllis Kahn and Senate author Gary Laidig look on.

SEAFOOD & MOREL OMELETTE

Yield: 4 to 6 servings

1/2 pound shelled prawns or shrimp
3/4 pound morels, sliced
18 oysters or mussels, shelled
2 cups MOREL SAUCE (see INDEX)
12 eggs
Butter
Salt
Pepper
Mix shrimp or prawns, morels and oysters or mussels. Bind together with one cup MOREL SAUCE. Gently heat. Make omelet(s) in the usual way with eggs, butter and seasonings.

Place filling in the center. Pour remaining MOREL SAUCE around the omelet.

STUFFED EGGPLANT

Yield: 2 servings

1 eggplant
1/4 pound morels
2 tablespoons butter
1/4 cup onion, minced
1/8 cup bread crumbs
Parmesan cheese, freshly grated

Parboi l eggplant for 20 minutes. Split in half lengthwise. Remove the inside and chop it up. Sauté morels in butter for three minutes and, just before they're done, add minced onion. Mix the mushrooms with the chopped eggplant and return into the two halves. Sprinkle lightly with bread crumbs, parmesan cheese, and dab with a little butter. Bake at a pre-heated 350 degrees for 20 minutes.

The composition of most edible wild   mushrooms is similar:
90 % water
3% protein
Small amounts of carbohydrates, fats and vitamins.

Ancient Romans thought of mushrooms as food for the gods and denied them even to themselves except on festive occasions and state banquets..

Z's STUFFED MORELS

Yield: about 20 mushrooms

1 pound morels
1/2 pound chicken or veal, pre-cooked
1/2 cup cracker crumbs
2 tablespoons butter or margarine
1/2 teaspoon salt
1/4 teaspoon pepper

Preheat oven to 400 degrees. Clean and dry morels. Split the stems only. Set aside. Finely chop chicken or veal, mix with cracker crumbs, butter or margarine, salt and pepper. Stuff caps with mixture. Pinch or tie stems together. Place in covered dish with one teaspoon water. Bake until tender, about 15 minutes.

Even though many mushrooms flourish in caves, cellars and in the woods, they contain a lot of vitamin D, the sunshine vitamin.

ZUCCHINI & CARROT STUFFED MORELS

Yield: about 15 mushrooms

12 ounces morels
1/4 cup salad oil
1 tablespoon vinegar
1/4 teaspoon salt
1/4 teaspoon basil leaves, crushed
1/8 teaspoon garlic powder
1/2 cup shredded carrot
1/2 cup shredded zucchini

Rinse morels and pat dry. Remove stems (use in soups, stews, sauces, etc.). Cook caps in boiled salted water about three minutes. Remove with slotted spoon and drain. Set aside to cool. Cover and refrigerate. In small bowl combine oil, vinegar, salt, basil and garlic powder. Mix in carrot and zucchini. Cover and refrigerate at least three hours or overnight. Spoon one tablespoon zucchini mixture into each mushroom cap. Place on baking sheet and cook at 400 degrees for ten minutes.

Wild mushrooms exude more liquid when exposed to heat than cultivated ones.

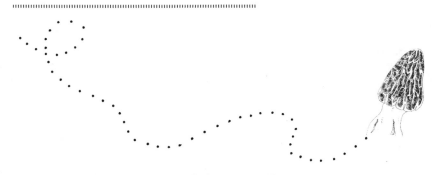

ZUCCHINI & MOREL CASSEROLE

Yield: 6 servings

1 pound zucchini, trimmed and scrubbed
1 pinch dill, fresh chopped or dried
clove garlic
2 Boiling salt water
1/2 pound morels, sliced
tablespoons butter
2 tablespoons flour
1 cup sour cream
Buttered bread crumbs

Cut zucchini crosswise into one-inch slices, add dill and garlic and enough boiling salted water cover, and return to a boil. Reduce heat, cover simmer gently until zucchini is tender. Do not overcook. Drain, reserving two tablespoons of cooking liquid. Discard the garlic.

Sauté the morels in butter five minutes, stirring occasionally. Stir in the flour and cook two minutes longer. Add the sour cream, zucchini and reserved cooking liquid, stirring constantly. Correct the seasonings and heat thoroughly but do not boil.

Transfer the mixture to a casserole and top with buttered bread crumbs. Brown quickly under high broiler heat.

V.

Sauces & Soups

BOULLION MOREL SOUP

Yield: 4 servings

1/2 cup onion, chopped
1/4 cup butter or margarine
1 pound morels, sliced
1 tablespoon all-purpose flour
3/4 cup water
1 chicken bouillon cube
1/4 teaspoon salt
1/4 teaspoon basil, crushed
1 dash bottled hot pepper sauce

Cook onion in butter until tender but not brown. Add morels and flour, toss to coat. Stir in water, bouillon cube, salt, basil and hot pepper sauce. Cook, stirring constantly, until mixture boils. Simmer 8 to 10 minutes, stirring occasionally. Serve piping hot.

CREAM OF MOREL SOUP

Yield: 4 to 6 servings

1 pound morels
Juice of one lemon
6 tablespoons butter
2 tablespoons onion, chopped
1 small clove garlic, chopped
Salt
Pepper
5 tablespoons flour
4-1/2 cups beef stock
1/2 cup heavy cream

Chop morels finely. Sprinkle with lemon juice. Melt 1/3 of the butter in a pan and cook the onion and garlic in it until soft and yellow, but not brown. Add morels and cook until juices are absorbed by mushrooms. Season to taste with salt and pepper.

Meanwhile, melt the remaining butter in a large saucepan. Stir in the flour then add hot beef stock gradually, stirring all the time to avoid lumps. Simmer 20 minutes. Add the mushroom mixture and simmer an additional 10 minutes. Correct seasonings. Add cream. Serve very hot.

Mushrooms are great diet fare. The average button mushroom has 124 calories per pound. Morels have 90.

First Lady of Michigan, Paula Blanchard, meets with author Larry Lonik and Rep. Tom Alley (D-West Branch), to talk about making the morel Michigan's state mushroom.

CREAMY MOREL GRAVY

Yield: 2 cups

2 cups milk
4 tablespoons all-purpose flour
1/4 cup morels, finely chopped
1 tablespoon butter
Salt (dash)
Pepper (dash)

Sauté chopped morels lightly in butter. After about 2 minutes morels will turn "soupy". Remove from heat then. In a screw-top jar shake flour with half the milk, salt and pepper until blended. Stir into morels. Add remaining milk. Cook, stirring constantly, until thick and bubbly. Cook 2 to 3 minutes longer.

FRESH MOREL SOUP

Yield: 10 servings

3 tablespoons vegetable oil
1-1/2 cups onions, peeled, chopped
1 cup chopped leeks (or green onions or scallions)
1/4 cup uncooked converted long-grain white rice
3/4 pound morels, sliced
6 cups canned or homemade chicken broth
2 cups water
1/2 teaspoon salt
1/8 teaspoon ground pepper

In a 3 quart saucepan heat oil over moderately high heat. Add onion and leek. Cook 3-4 minutes, stirring frequently, until soft but not brown. Add rice and mushrooms and cook two minutes longer, stirring frequently. Add remaining ingredients; cover and simmer 20 minutes, until rice is tender. Remove from heat and put one cup of the soup mixture into a blender. Cover and blend 40 seconds at low speed, until pureed. Pour into a large bowl and repeat with remaining soup. Pour pureed soup back into pan and heat over moderately low heat until hot. Serve.

The ancient Greek physician Discorides, noted that poisonous fungi grew either among rusty nails or rotten rags, near serpents' holes or trees that produced noxious fruits..

A typical spore is a single thin-walled cell about 1/2500 of an inch long.

MIKULA'S POTATO & MOREL SOUP

Yield: 10 servings

5 tablespoons butter (divided)
2 leeks, chopped
2 large carrots, chopped
6 cups chicken broth
2 teaspoons dill weed
2 teaspoons salt
5 cups peeled, diced potatoes
1 pound morels, sliced
1 cup half and half
2 tablespoons flour

In large kettle, sauté leeks and carrots in three tablespoons butter until soft, about five minutes. Stir in chicken broth, dill, salt and potatoes. Bring to a boil, reduce heat and simmer until potatoes are just tender, about 20 minutes. Meanwhile, melt remaining 2 tablespoons butter in a skillet. Add mushrooms and sauté until golden brown. Stir together flour and half and half. Add, along with mushrooms, to soup. Cook, stirring constantly until mixture thickens and comes to a boil. Serve.

MOREL BISQUE

Yield: about 2 quarts

1   pound fresh morels
1   quart chicken broth
1   medium onion, chopped
7   tablespoons butter
6   tablespoons flour
3   cups milk
1   cup heavy cream
teaspoon (or more) salt
White pepper
Tabasco sauce
2   tablespoons Sherry (optional)

Wash morels and cut off stems. Slice 6 caps and reserve. Grind or chop the remaining caps and stems very fine. Simmer, covered, in the broth with the onion for thirty minutes.

Sauté the reserved sliced morel caps in one tablespoon of butter and reserve for garnish.

Melt the remaining butter in a saucepan, add the flour and stir with a wire whisk until blended. Meanwhile, bring the milk to a boil and add all at once to the butter-flour mixture, stirring vigorously with the whisk until the sauce is thickened and smooth. Add the cream.

Combine the mushroom-broth mixture with the sauce and season to taste with salt, pepper and Tabasco sauce.

Reheat and add the sherry before serving. Garnish with sautéed mushrooms.

MOREL PUREE

Yield: 4 to 6 servings

1   pound morels, sliced Juice of 1/2 lemon
8   tablespoons butter
3   tablespoons chicken broth Pepper (pinch)
Grated nutmeg (pinch)
1   cup fresh white breadcrumbs Heavy cream
1/3 cup half and half

Lightly blanch morels for three minutes in some water and the lemon juice. Drain and chop morels, then cook them gently in half the butter for 10 minutes. Add chicken broth, pepper and nutmeg and continue to cook, covered, for 20 more minutes. Mix bread crumbs to a paste with some heavy cream. Add to mushroom mixture over low heat, stirring constantly, until all is blended and heated through.

Kids make great mushroom hunters. They're lower to the ground, have better eyesight, and lots more energy.

MOREL SAUCE WITH PASTA

Yield: 2 to 3 servings

1/2 pound morels, sliced
2   tablespoons lemon juice
1   small onion (or shallot), chopped
1   large clove garlic, chopped
4   tablespoons butter
4   tablespoons olive oil
1   bunch parsley, chopped Salt
Pepper

Sprinkle morels with lemon juice. Cook onion or shallot and garlic gently in the butter and oil until they soften, without browning. Add morels and parsley, raising heat slightly, and cook 10 more minutes. Season to taste with salt and pepper.

The Elusive Morel

Commercial mushrooming utilizes a number of environments, including abandoned mines, limestone caves, sheltered quarries and other types of caves.

The Chinese word for "morel", when translated, means "sheep's stomach".

MOREL SAUCE FOR ROASTS AND PAN-FRIED MEAT

Yield: 4 to 6 servings

1/2 pound morels, chopped
6 shallots, minced
6 tablespoons butter
2-1/2 tablespoons flour
2/3 cup dry white wine
1-1/4 cups meat stock
1/4 cup canned tomato sauce
 Meat juices from roasting pan or frying pan
Salt
Pepper
Parsley, chopped
Tarragon
Chervil

Brown mushrooms and shallots lightly in half the butter Stir in flour, then add wine, stock and tomato sauce. Cook 15 to 20 minutes until the flavor and texture are rich. Add more tomato sauce if desired. After meat has been roasted or fried, skim off the fat and add juices to the sauce. Remove from heat. Mix in remaining butter Season to taste with salt and pepper. Add herbs Serve immediately.

In Europe, more than a dozen species of <u>Morchella</u> have been described.

The philosopher Horace said that fungi that grew in meadows were best.

MOREL SAUCE SUPREME

Yield: 3 cups
2 ounces (4 tablespoons) butter
2-1/2 tablespoons flour
1-1/4 cups chicken stock
2 ounces morels, chopped
1-1/3 cups heavy cream
2 egg yolks
Salt
Pepper

Melt butter and stir in flour. Heat the stock, add it and mix until smooth. Add morels and simmer steadily for a minimum of 10 minutes. Gradually stir in the cream. Beat egg yolks, add a little sauce and add to pan. Thicken without boiling, over moderate heat. Salt and pepper to taste.

MOREL WINE SAUCE

Yield: 6 servings

2 tablespoons butter
1 tablespoon parsley, chopped
1/2 clove garlic, finely chopped
1 small onion, chopped
1 tablespoon flour
1 cup chicken broth
1/8 teaspoon nutmeg
3/4 pound morels, thinly sliced
1/4 cup dry sherry

In a saucepan heat one tablespoon of the butter Add parsley, garlic and onion Cook over medium heat three minutes. Stir in flour. Gradually add broth, stirring constantly. Add nutmeg.

In a skillet heat the remaining butter. Add morels and sauté five minutes. Combine with the sauce and simmer fifteen minutes. Add wine and bring to a boil. Serve with roast meats or poultry.

In the Middle Ages the king bolete mushroom, a nutty-flavored delicacy, had to be turned over to the local prince (royalty) if found – by law.

Mycophagy is the eating of wild mushrooms.

MUSHROOM SAUCE

Yield: 3 cups

5 tablespoons butter, divided
1/2 pound morels, sliced
2 tablespoons onion, chopped
1 small clove garlic, chopped
2-1/2 tablespoons flour
1 1/4 cups chicken stock
1-1/4 cups milk
Salt
 Cayenne pepper

Melt 4 tablespoons butter. At medium heat cook morels five minutes. Add onion and garlic. Cover and cook five more minutes. Stir in flour, add stock and milk. Leave to simmer a minimum of ten minutes. Season to taste. Just before serving, mix in remaining tablespoon of butter.

In 1984, the Indiana Horticulture Society reported that production of morels in the state of Indiana was between 50,000 and 100,000 bushels.

PRIMERO MOREL BISQUE

Yield: 6-8 servings

1/4 cup sweet butter
1 small onion, chopped
1/2 cup celery, chopped
3/4 pound morels, sliced
1 medium-size potato, peeled and diced
1 cup water
1 teaspoon salt
3/4 teaspoon fresh, minced thyme (or 1/4 teaspoon dried)
1 pinch freshly ground white pepper
2 cups milk
3/4 cup heavy cream
1/4 cup Amontillado Sherry
2 teaspoons soy sauce

Melt butter in 6- to 8-quart Dutch Oven over medium-low heat. Add onion and celery Cover and cook until transparent, about ten minutes, stirring occasionally.

Stir in mushrooms and cook until tender, about five minutes. Add potato, water, salt, thyme and pepper. Increase heat and simmer until potato is very soft, about 15 minutes.

Puree the mixture in food processor or blender until smooth, stopping occasionally to scrape down sides of the container. Return mixture to saucepan Add milk, cream, sherry and soy sauce. Heat through, but do not boil. Serve hot or chilled. (Suggested garnish - sour cream)

RUSSIAN SOUR CREAM & MOREL SAUCE

Yield: about 2 cups

1 onion, chopped
3/4 pound morels, chopped
3 tablespoons butter
1 tablespoon flour
1 cup sour cream
Dillweed or fennel, chopped
Salt
Pepper

Cook mushrooms, then onions in butter, about 10 minutes each. Combine and stir in flour. Leave for 5 minutes at low heat. Add sour cream, gradually. When cream begins to come to a boil sauce is done. Add dill or fennel to taste, then salt and pepper.

Sewing morels together and hanging them to dry in the sun and air is a great way to preserve your surplus mushrooms, if you' re lucky to have a surplus.

WHITE WINE SAUCE FOR FISH OR CHICKEN

Yield: 4 to 6 servings

1/2 pound morels, chopped
4 tablespoons butter
1-1/4 cups fish stock
2 tablespoons lemon juice
2 tablespoons flour
1 cup white wine
2 egg yolks
 Salt
 Pepper
Sugar (pinch)
 2/3 cup heavy cream

Cook morels for five minutes in half the butter. Add about half the fish stock and the lemon juice. Leave to simmer for 20 minutes without lid on pan. Meanwhile melt the remaining butter in another pan, stir in flour, the rest of the fish stock and the wine. Allow to cook down a few minutes. Beat the egg yolks in a bowl. Quickly add the almost-boiling wine sauce bit by bit. Clean cooking pan out and put an inch of water in it. When simmering, stand the bowl of sauce over it and stir gently until it thickens Do not allow to boil. Add the mushrooms and season with salt and pepper. If you are using dry wine add just a pinch of sugar. Stir in the cream. Continue cooking until the sauce is very hot.

For chicken substitute chicken stock for fish stock. Some chopped fresh tarragon can be added at the end.

Index

A

I am always looking for more information (unusual experiences, recipes, mushroom- and nature-related activities, photos, drawings, picking times in all areas, hot spots, tall tales, etc.). Please write or email me c/o the publisher....

RKT Publishing   PO Box 172   Chelsea,   MI 48118

Email: tree@morelheaven.com

www.morelheaven.com

Check out the website for personal appearance schedules, photos, new stuff and more mushroom fun.

Best wishes and good hunting always!

"Tree"

MORE FUN WITH NATURE AND COOKING

**BASICALLY MORELS : MUSHROOM HUNTING, COOK-
ING, LORE & ADVICE** (Larry Lonik). The book that started
it all--now updated and revised from cover to cover. The whos,
whats, wheres, whens, whys and hows of successful morel hunting and cooking (60 recipes--from campfire basics to gourmet
kitchen). Preservation tips, mushroom clubs, festivals & much
more. The first and most popular book of its kind, and easily the
most fun – now even better! 144 pages. 6 X 9.   B/W photos,
illustrations. *$11.95.*

SPECIALTY MUSHROOMS, SPECIAL RECIPES (Larry
Lonik). Morel, bolete, chanterelle, shiitake, portabello,
matsutake, oyster, truffle, black trumpet, enoki, porcini
and maitake – wonderful mushrooms that one can find in
the forests and at specialty suppliers. Fabulous gourmet
recipes (60). Inside "scoops" on where and when to find
these mushrooms, mushroom cultivation, mushroom
hunting tips, humous stories and more. 160 pages. 6X9.
32 pages of beautiful full COLOR photos. B/W photos,
illustrations. *$14.95.*

**MORELS: TRUE OR FALSE: THE ESSENTIAL FIELD
GUIDE & MORE** (Larry Lonik). Finally, an easy-to-use, up-
to-date Field Guide that clearly shows the good and the bad, and
how to tell them apart. Full COLOR photos of the seven most
common "morels" one can encounter in the Spring – in their natural habitat and cross-sectioned. The latest and most accurate information -- from the World's No. 1 morel expert! With all the
widespread (surely unintentional) bad info out there, an absolute
MUST. Plus a unique question/answer section that will make
your mushroom experiences safer and more productive, whether
you're a novice or a seasoned pro. 80 pages.   6 X 9. 32 pages
of COLOR photos. B/W photos, illustrations. *$11.95*

THE HEALTHY TASTE OF HONEY: BEE PEOPLE'S RECIPES, ANECDOTES & LORE (Larry Lonik). Amazing facts about bees, honey, pollen, beeswax, beekeeping, history, medicine, health, and humor.... Plus over 150 delicious recipes in a variety of categories. Did you know when they dug up King Tut's tomb they found honey that was still edible? Learn and enjoy. Bee healthy! 170 pages. 6 X 9. B/W photos, illustrations. *$11.95.*

MOREL MUSHROOM HUNTING VIDEO. COLOR 60 minutes. As seen on PBS. Everything you ever wanted to know, see or hear about morels. *$19.95.*

MOREL COOKING VIDEO. COLOR. 60 minutes. From the campsite to the gourmet kitchen. Basic all-time favorites plus a taste of the exotic. Special guest, internationally-heralded chef Tom MacKinnon. Seen on PBS. *$19.95.*

MOTHERLODE VIDEO. COLOR. 38 minutes. The ultimate morel film. Amazing "squirrel Cam" cinematography. Tons of morels. Mind-boggling – and hilarious too! A classic forever. $19.95.

TO ORDER:
By mail: Send check or money order to:
  RKT PUBLISHING
   PO Box 172
   Chelsea, MI 48118
Include a list of items you want and your return address.
Add a $4.00 flat fee (shipping and handling) for any size order.
Order online from our website:
www.morelheaven.com

ABOUT THE AUTHOR

Naturalist Larry Lonik is a man of many interests. He has been successful in the business world, draws and paints, composes and performs music and has created for educational television and motion pictures. BASICALLY MORELS is Larry's fifth book in his Nature/ Cooking series, which began with THE HEALTHY TASTE OF HONEY, first published in 1981.

He has produced videos on Mushroom Hunting and Cooking that have aired on PBS. He's appeared on CNN, National Public Radio, many TV and radio shows, been active with seminars, guided mushroom hunts and cooking demonstrations. He was a primary player at Morel Mountain and Mr. Mushroom, two breakthrough companies that grew morels commercially. He's currently doing research with mushrooms for arthritis and cancer.

Larry is fascinated with the application of scientific principles to Man and his environment. "The answers are right in front of us — what we are, where we came from... how to be productive, efficient, effective, healthy and happy." The 6-foot 7-inch native of Michigan (nicknamed "Tree") and graduate of Michigan State University combined 25 years of research (personal study, interviews with botanists, mycologists, chefs, public officials and countless morel enthusiasts) with 45 years of personal mushroom picking, eating and growing experience to produce the latest trio of BASICALLY MORELS, MORELS: TRUE OR FALSE and SPECIALTY MUSHROOMS, SPECIAL RECIPES.

Back cover photo: Author Lonik takes a break during a particularly strenuous mushroom hunt, with his dogs, King and Crimson, in a field of wild leeks.